T0114594

William H. Rehnquist

CENTENNIAL CRISIS

William H. Rehnquist was born in Milwaukee, Wisconsin, and served in the U.S. Army Air Corps during World War II. He earned his B.A. and M.A. in political science from Stanford University and a second M.A. from Harvard. He graduated first in his class at Stanford Law School in 1952. In 1969 Rehnquist became assistant attorney general for the Justice Department's Office of Legal Council. He was confirmed by the Senate as an associate justice of the Supreme Court in December 1971 and took his place on the bench in January 1972. He became the sixteenth Chief Justice of the Supreme Court in 1986. He lives in Arlington, Virginia.

ALSO BY WILLIAM H. REHNQUIST

The Supreme Court: New Edition

All the Laws but One

*Grand Inquests: The Historical Impeachments of Justice Samuel Chase
and President Andrew Johnson*

CENTENNIAL CRISIS

CENTENNIAL
CRISIS

THE DISPUTED ELECTION OF 1876

William H. Rehnquist

VINTAGE BOOKS
A DIVISION OF RANDOM HOUSE, INC.
NEW YORK

FIRST VINTAGE BOOKS EDITION, JANUARY 2005

The Library of Congress has cataloged the Knopf edition as follows:
Rehnquist, William H.
Centennial Crisis / William H. Rehnquist.—1st ed.
p. cm.
Includes bibliographical references and index.
1. Presidents—United States—Election—1876.   2. Contested elections—United
States—History—19th century.   3. Elections—Corrupt practices—United States—
History—19th century.   4. Political corruption—United States—History—19th
century.   5. United States—Politics and government—1869–1877.   6. Hayes,
Rutherford Birchard, 1822–1893.   7. Tilden, Samuel J. (Samuel Jones), 1814–1886.
8. Presidential candidates—United States—Biography.   9. Bradley, Joseph P.,
1813–1892.   10. Judges—United States—Biography.   I. Title.
E680.R44   2004
324.973'082—dc22
2003059630

Vintage ISBN: 978-0-375-71321-7

Author photograph © Dane Penland, Smithsonian
Book design by Robert C. Olsson

www.vintagebooks.com

Contents

List of Illustrations

List of Illustrations

Acknowledgments

I dedicate this book to Charles Fairman, who first introduced me to the Supreme Court in an undergraduate course in Constitutional Law at Stanford University. His published work in the era of the Court with which this book deals has been an important source for it.

My daughter, Nancy Spears, has been my editor of first resort in the preparation of the book and has made many useful suggestions. My editor at Alfred A. Knopf, Pat Hass, has again expertly sought out unnecessary verbiage in my draft, and the book is the better for it.

My secretaries, Janet Tramonte and Laverne Frayer, have typed the manuscript, and my aide, Joe Mullaney, has assisted me in a number of different ways. The Library of the Supreme Court of the United States, headed by Librarian Shelley Dowling, Patricia McCabe, Linda Maslow, Katherine Romano, and Sara Sonet of the Library staff. In gathering photographs for the book, Katherine Fitts, Curator of the Supreme Court, and Franz Jantzen have both helped greatly in obtaining hard-to-get photographs. My friend Peter McKay, because of his interest in the subject, has furnished helpful suggestions.

CENTENNIAL CRISIS

— PROLOGUE —

THE DISPUTED ELECTION of 2000, in which Florida's electoral votes made Republican George W. Bush President instead of Democrat Al Gore, was the subject of intense media coverage: on network news, in daily newspapers, and in weekly news magazines. In this coverage, there was an occasional brief reference to another disputed presidential election: the 1876 contest between Republican Rutherford B. Hayes and Democrat Samuel Tilden. But to most Americans who have not majored in American history in college, the earlier race was at best a long-forgotten episode briefly mentioned in a high school civics text.

There were undoubted similarities between the two events. The very fact that the outcome of a presidential election would be uncertain for weeks after the polling day was one. The Constitution provides that the decision be made by electors chosen in the states in November, who don't cast their votes until December. But in normal presidential elections, the voting of the electors is a formality, predetermined by the popular vote cast in each state on the first Tuesday of November. Only when the issue of which candidate won the popular vote in a state arises does the choice of electors become controversial.

Twice in our history the chosen electors did not give a majority of their votes to a single candidate: in 1800, when Thomas Jefferson and Aaron Burr each received the same number of votes, and in 1824, when the electors divided their votes among several candidates. In each of these instances, as the Constitution provided, the election of the President was thrown into the House of Representatives. The result was that Thomas Jefferson became President in 1801, and John Quincy Adams did so in 1825. But the only times that there was a dispute as to which slate of electors had been chosen in a particular state were 1876 and 2000.

There were other similarities. In each case, a two-term incumbent was stepping down from the office of President: Republican U. S. Grant in 1876, and Democrat Bill Clinton in 2000. Each of the years was special for reasons other than the occurrence of the presidential election. The year 2000 was regarded by many as a millennial year, with appropriate worldwide celebration on January 1. Eighteen seventy-six was the centennial year of the United States as a nation—the Declaration of Independence had been adopted a century earlier. Excited crowds in Philadelphia on New Year's Eve, 1875, vowed that even if Congress would not appropriate the funds, Pennsylvania would finance the forthcoming Centennial Exhibition in Philadelphia.

There were significant differences, too. In 1876 there was no NATO, no United Nations, no Balkan or Mideastern crisis that concerned the United States. This country was more than a week away from Europe by steamship—the fastest known means of ocean transportation—and more than twice that distance from Asian countries such as Japan and China.

There were no serious current disputes with either of our continental neighbors, Mexico and Canada. During our Civil War, French Emperor Louis Napoléon had taken advantage of the United States' preoccupation with fighting to impose upon Mexico as its ruler Maximilian, brother of Emperor Franz Josef of Austria. As soon as the Civil War was over, Secretary of State William Seward pressed France to withdraw its troops supporting this puppet. It did, Maximillian was overthrown, and Porfirio Díaz, a Mexican, came to power.

While there had once been support in the United States for the idea of annexing Canada—a sentiment not shared by many Canadians—that support had receded. In 1867, the British Parliament passed the British North America Act, which gave Canada a considerable measure of self-government and a parliament of its own. The United States came to realize that Canada was here to stay.

It was well that there were no current international crises concerning the United States, because the country did not know for certain until March 2, 1877—two days before the inauguration date at that time—that Hayes would be the new President. That was because of the complicated machinery that Congress devised after the dispute over the returns crystallized. The Democrats had a majority in the House of Representatives, and the Republicans in the Senate. The passage of any measure therefore required the support of both parties, and ultimately of the candidates themselves. Congress created an Electoral Commission, composed of five congressional Democrats, five congressional Republicans, and five members of the United States Supreme Court, to make what was in effect a final determination as to which returns from Florida, South Carolina, Louisiana, and Oregon would be counted.

This was quite different from the resolution process in the disputed election of 2000, in which the Supreme Court of the United States and the supreme court of Florida were the principal postelection actors. There was profound dissatisfaction with the process on the part of the losing parties in both 2000 and 1876. Perhaps when such a dispute erupts, there is no means of resolving it that will satisfy both sides. But for all of those whose interest in the process of electing a President was quickened by the disputed election of 2000, a review of what happened in 1876 should be interesting and perhaps instructive. To that review, this book is dedicated.

— CHAPTER 1 —

O<small>N</small> M<small>AY</small> 10, 1876, the Centennial Exhibition, commemorating one hundred years of American independence, opened in Philadelphia—the logical place to hold such an exhibition. It was there on July 4, 1776, that the Continental Congress adopted the Declaration of Independence, proclaiming in Thomas Jefferson's stirring words that "these united colonies are, and of Right ought to be, Free and Independent States."

Philadelphia in 1776 was not only the seat of the rudimentary national government, but also the largest city in the country. After the ratification of the Constitution in 1789, Philadelphia became the temporary capital of the infant nation, but in 1800 lost out to the new city of Washington as the site of the permanent seat of government. In time New York overtook Philadelphia as the most populous city, and both New York and Boston became more prominent centers of commerce on the East Coast. But Philadelphia rose to the occasion in 1876. Two hundred buildings were constructed in Fairmount Park, and on opening day more than 186,000 people visited the grounds. Many foreign nations took buildings to exhibit their cultures and accomplishments. Fukui Makota, the Japanese commissioner to the exposition, observed:

> The first day crowds come like sheep, run here, run there, run everywhere. One man start, one thousand follow. Nobody can see anything, nobody can do anything. All rush, push, tear, shout, make plenty noise, say damn great many times, get very tired, and go home.[1]

When the exhibition closed six months later, it had been visited by more than 10 million people. It was truly the first man-made tourist mecca in the United States.

Much had changed in the first century of America's existence. In the eighteenth century, travel by land was either on foot or horseback, or in a vehicle drawn by horse or oxen. Travel by water was accomplished by sailing vessels. But in 1806, Robert Fulton invented the steamboat, and by 1830 the first railroads were being built in the United States. Transportation was revolutionized. Samuel F. B. Morse invented the telegraph in 1843; Cyrus McCormick followed with the mechanical reaper, and Elias Howe with the sewing machine. In 1869 the transcontinental railroad was completed with the driving of the Golden Spike at Promontory Point, Utah. And in the very year of the centennial, Alexander Graham Bell would patent the telephone.

The nation had also grown spectacularly in size. The Louisiana Purchase in 1803 added the territory between the Mississippi River and the Rocky Mountains, and the cession following the Mexican War added the Southwest. Colorado was admitted to the Union in 1876 as the thirty-eighth state; it would be known as the Centennial State.

On the exhibition's opening day President and Mrs. U. S. Grant, accompanied by the Brazilian Emperor Dom Pedro and his wife, Theresa, were among the notables present. At the scheduled time the President and the Emperor opened the valves that started a huge steam engine in Machinery Hall. The steam engine in turn supplied power to hundreds of other machines at the fair. When the wheels began to turn, guns roared, church bells pealed, and whistles blew. The fair, and the Centennial, had officially begun.

Grant was in the last year of his second term as President. Elected in 1868 and reelected in 1872, he was the second Republican President; Lincoln, of course, was the first. In the two decades since its founding, the party had achieved a remarkable success. The event that precipitated its founding was the enactment by Congress of the Kansas–Nebraska Act in 1854.

In that year Stephen A. Douglas, an able and ambitious Democratic senator from Illinois introduced in the Senate a bill providing for what he called "popular sovereignty"—and what his opponents called "squatter sovereignty"—to determine whether or not the territories of Kansas and Nebraska should allow slavery within their borders. This bill aroused instant opposition among antislavery forces in the North, because it repealed a portion of the Missouri Compromise, which Congress had enacted in 1820.

The Missouri Compromise came about when both Maine and Missouri sought admission to the Union as states. Maine would be a free state with no slavery, and Missouri would be a slave state. The Missouri Compromise admitted both states, and went on to provide that thereafter slavery would be prohibited in all territories of the United States north of the southern border of Missouri. Since both Kansas and Nebraska were north of this line, Douglas' Kansas–Nebraska Act would repeal that portion of the Missouri Compromise.

After fierce debate, the bill passed both houses of Congress and was signed by President Franklin Pierce. But the antagonism aroused in the North had a lasting effect on national politics. Douglas himself, after he toured the North following the adjournment of Congress, said he could have traveled from Boston to Chicago by the light of the fires kindled to burn him in effigy.

Early in 1854, a meeting was held in a schoolhouse in Ripon, Wisconsin, to oppose the extension of slavery. This led to a state convention in Madison in July which adopted the name "Republican" for the new party. A week earlier a state convention in Jackson, Michigan, adopted the same name for the new party in that state.

The fledgling party held a national convention in Philadelphia in 1856 and nominated John C. Frémont as its candidate for President. His Democratic opponent was James Buchanan, a long-time officeholder who had been absent as minister to England during the furor over the Kansas–Nebraska Act. In the election that fall, Buchanan carried every slave state but Maryland, together with Indiana, Illinois, and his home state of Pennsylvania. All of the other northern states voted for Frémont. He polled 1.34 million popular votes, losing to Buchanan, who polled 1.8 million votes.

Two days after Buchanan was inaugurated in March 1857, the Supreme Court handed down its ill-starred decision in the Dred Scott case, holding that the limitation of slavery effected by the Missouri Compromise was unconstitutional. This decision further inflamed northern opinion. The following year Stephen Douglas came up for reelection as United States senator in Illinois. He was opposed by Abraham Lincoln on the Republican ticket. They debated at seven different towns in downstate Illinois, thrashing out the question, among others, of the expansion of slavery. At that time senators were elected by the state legislatures rather than by popular vote. The Democrats narrowly retained control of the Illinois legislature, and in January 1859, it duly reelected Douglas.

Two years later, Lincoln and Douglas again battled each other, but this time the prize was the presidency of the United States. Douglas was not sufficiently proslavery for the southern wing of the Democratic Party, and it nominated John Breckenridge on a ticket which ran only in the South. The northern Democrats nominated Douglas. A fourth party—the Constitutional Union party—sought to ignore the issue of slavery entirely and was on the ballot in only the border states. The Republican Party was almost entirely northern in its appeal, opposing as it did any further extension of slavery in the territories.

On election day—November 6, 1860—Lincoln was elected President with a majority of the electoral votes—all of them from northern states—but only a minority of the popular vote. Even before he was inaugurated the following March, the seven states of the Deep South seceded and formed the Confederate States of America. In April 1861, the Confederate shore batteries in the harbor of Charleston, South Carolina, opened fire on the small Union garrison at Fort Sumter on an island in the harbor. The garrison surrendered the following day, and Lincoln called for 75,000 volunteers to put down the rebellion. The Civil War had begun.

At the outbreak of the Civil War, thirty-nine-year-old Ulysses S. Grant had been a clerk in a leather store operated by two of his brothers in the Mississippi River town of Galena, Illinois. Grant had graduated from West Point with an undistinguished record, and served in the Mexican War and at Army posts in the United States until 1854, when he resigned his commission. For the next

Justice Nathan Clifford, painted in 1967 from earlier portraits.

seven years, he was a farmer, a real-estate agent, a candidate for county engineer, and a clerk in a customs house. In none of these occupations was he particularly successful.

After Lincoln's call for volunteers, Grant was appointed by Illinois Governor Richard Yates to be a colonel in one of the Illinois volunteer regiments. Grant led the forces which successfully captured first Fort Henry on the Tennessee River and then Fort Donelson on the Cumberland River. He commanded Union forces at the Battle of Shiloh, and then successfully invested the southern fortress of Vicksburg, Mississippi. Vicksburg fell on July 4, 1863, thereby cutting the Confederacy in two from north to south.

Grant was promoted to major general in the regular Army. After commanding Union troops at the Battle of Lookout Mountain, he was promoted to General in Chief of the Union forces. He devised a plan to employ all of his numerically superior troops against the enemy, correctly theorizing that if he could keep the losses even, the Union forces would prevail. Battling in Virginia from the spring of 1864 until Lee's surrender at Appomattox in April 1865, Grant was the Union hero of the Civil War.

During the summer of 1864, there was considerable war-weariness in states such as Ohio, Illinois, and Indiana. The war had lasted longer than most anyone expected, and Union losses were heavy in battles such as the Wilderness and Cold Harbor. Salmon P. Chase, Lincoln's Secretary of the Treasury, mounted a stealthy but unsuccessful campaign to obtain the Republican presidential nomination himself. But Lincoln easily won renomination at the party convention in Baltimore in June. The Democrats met in Chicago in August and adopted a "peace plank" in their platform. This plank called for an immediate cease-fire and a negotiated peace. They nominated General George McClellan for President, whose first act after accepting the nomination was to repudiate the peace plank.

Fate smiled on the Republicans as the election drew closer. In September, the city of Atlanta fell to General William T. Sherman after a long siege. Admiral David Farragut won the important naval battle of Mobile Bay. In November, Lincoln was reelected by a margin of more than two to one in the popular vote.

Five days after Lee surrendered to Grant at Appomattox, Lincoln was assassinated by John Wilkes Booth at Ford's Theater. He was succeeded by Vice President Andrew Johnson, with whom Grant had nothing like the close relationship that he had developed with Lincoln. Grant was now Commander in Chief of a rapidly demobilizing army, and a popular hero.

Johnson would try to carry out Lincoln's conciliatory approach to the seceded states, but soon ran into conflict with the Radical Republicans who would dominate Congress after 1866. He successively vetoed civil rights bills and Reconstruction bills, only to have his vetoes overridden by Congress. He was finally impeached in 1868 after he removed his disloyal Secretary of War, Edwin M. Stanton, from office. The trial in the Senate in the spring of 1868 lasted many weeks; Johnson was finally acquitted by a margin of one vote. The proceedings in the Senate were adjourned to allow the Republicans to attend their national convention in Chicago.

At that convention, Grant's was the only name placed in nomination for President, and he was unanimously chosen on the first ballot. Up until the Civil War, he had led a largely apolitical life. The only vote he cast for President was in 1856; he voted for Buchanan because, he said, "he knew Frémont." He would now run against Horatio Seymour, the Governor of New York, who was chosen by the Democrats after twenty-one exhausting ballots.

Seymour had publicly sympathized with draft rioters in New York during the war, and he was thought to have close ties to Wall Street bankers. This double burden was too much for him in a campaign against a war hero. Seymour carried only eight of the thirty-four states, and lost in the Electoral College by a margin of 214 to 80.

At forty-six, Grant was then the youngest President ever elected. He entered the presidency beholden to none of the political interests which are usually involved in the nominating process. He therefore had no political debts to pay when it came to cabinet positions or other appointments. In some ways this was an advantage; in others it was not. The historian Paul L. Haworth, writing almost a century ago, observed:

> Prior to |Grant's| nomination he had never held a civil office, and he did not really understand the workings of our political system. Starting out with the assumption that the Presidency was a sort of personal possession given him by the people to manage as he thought proper, he had, with the best intentions in the world, entirely ignored the party leaders in choosing his first cabinet.[2]

The downside of Grant's political naïveté was illustrated by his choices for the two most important cabinet offices—Secretary of State and Secretary of the Treasury. Grant nominated Elihu Washburne, an Illinois congressman from Galena, to be Secretary of State. Washburne was instrumental in obtaining a commission for Grant when he reentered the Army in 1861 but had no experience in foreign affairs. As it turned out, the permanent post he wanted was that of American minister to Paris (his wife was French), but he asked Grant as a favor to first appoint him Secretary of State. Grant obliged this bizarre request, Washburne resigned after a week in that office, and was duly appointed minister to Paris. Grant then nominated Hamilton Fish of New York to succeed Washburne. This choice commanded widespread public support, and Fish rendered highly competent service in that office for the entire eight years of Grant's presidency.

The President chose Alexander Stewart, a leading New York retailer, as Secretary of the Treasury, but senators pointed to a statute, first drafted by Alexander Hamilton, which forbade any person carrying on a business or trade to hold that office. Grant requested that the Senate exempt Stewart, but Charles Sumner of Massachusetts and Roscoe Conkling of New York both refused the request. Grant then acceded to Stewart's request that his name be withdrawn, and next selected Congressman George Boutwell of Massachusetts for the Treasury post.

Told that Pennsylvania, a populous and reliably Republican state, should be represented in his cabinet, Grant nominated Adolphe Borie of Philadelphia to be Secretary of the Navy. Borie's only connection with nautical matters was that he had retired from a successful career in the East India trade, but Grant had enjoyed his company while being entertained at Borie's Delaware estate.

The President chose Jacob D. Cox, ex-Governor of Ohio, as Secretary of the Interior, John Creswell of Maryland to be Postmaster General, and Ebenezer R. Hoar of Massachusetts to be Attorney General. All were recognized as able men and did not disappoint in their respective offices. Grant picked his longtime aide and military confidant General John Rawlins to be Secretary of War. Rawlins, however, was fatally ill with tuberculosis, and died within a few months.

GRANT collaborated with Fish to secure a major diplomatic triumph in the Treaty of Washington, approved in May 1871. It provided for arbitration of United States claims against Great

Britain resulting from the construction of Confederate warships in a British shipyard.

During the war, three Confederate warships—the *Alabama,* the *Florida,* and the *Shenandoah*—had been built in the Laird Shipyards in Liverpool. They wreaked havoc on Union shipping not only in the Atlantic Ocean but also in the Indian Ocean. The *Alabama* alone sank sixty-four vessels. The United States maintained that the British government was liable for the damage these warships inflicted on Union shipping. An attempt by Seward in the last days of the Johnson administration to settle the claims was overwhelmingly rejected by the Senate because it was thought prejudicial to the best interests of the United States.

In February 1871, the British government became more favorably inclined to settlement and sent five commissioners to join their American counterparts in Washington to draft a treaty. Secretary Fish was chairman of the American group, while the very able Englishman Lord Ripon chaired the British delegation. For two months, they worked diligently to come up with the mutually acceptable Treaty of Washington. It dealt with other issues outstanding between the two countries as well as the *Alabama* claims. With respect to the latter, it provided for submission to binding arbitration by a five-member tribunal to meet in Geneva, Switzerland. One member was to be appointed by Queen Victoria, one by President Grant, one by the King of Italy, one by the Emperor of Brazil, and the fifth by the President of the Swiss Confederation.

The treaty was a major milestone in relations between the United States and Great Britain, foreshadowing friendly relations for the indefinite future. The tribunal awarded the United States $15.5 million in damages for the depredations committed by the British warships. The proceedings brought to prominence

an unknown lawyer from Toledo, Ohio—Morrison R. Waite—
who was one of the attorneys representing the United States
before the tribunal. Two years later, Grant would appoint him
Chief Justice of the United States Supreme Court.

Grant also actively supported civil rights legislation. Members of the Ku Klux Klan in southern states were coming out in
force, intimidating and terrorizing Republican voters, many of
whom were black. Congress had passed two relatively mild
Enforcement Acts under the authority of the Civil War Amendments to the Constitution. But Klan violence and intimidation
continued in the election of 1870. When Congress convened in
March 1871, Grant requested legislation aimed directly at the
Klan. Some of the Republicans in Congress as well as Democrats
opposed the measure, saying that it would bring the federal government into an area traditionally reserved for the states. Federal
supervision of local affairs in the South was losing its appeal in
the North. But Grant was insistent and threw the full weight of
his office behind the bill, which would become known as the Ku
Klux Act. The bill made it a crime to conspire to prevent persons
from voting, holding office, or otherwise enjoying equal protection of the laws. It became law in April 1871 and was remarkably
effective, at least for the time, in curbing Klan violence in the
South.

Grant had other early successes; the first law he signed after
becoming President was entitled "An Act to Strengthen the Public Credit." It pledged the government to pay its bondholders in
gold and to redeem greenbacks "at the earliest practical period."
Secretary Boutwell began selling gold at weekly auctions, and the
amount of gold sold at these auctions had a significant influence
on the price of the metal on the New York market. The more
gold sold, the more difficult it would be to "corner" the market.
This worked well as long as no outsider knew in advance the

amount of gold the Treasury would sell each week. Boutwell was close-mouthed, and publicly announced his orders at the same time he telegraphed them to the assistant treasurer in New York who actually conducted the auction.

Two well-known "robber barons" of the era, Jay Gould and "Jubilee Jim" Fisk determined on a plan to corner the gold market. But to do so they needed someone on the inside of the administration to advise them of the government's decisions as to the amount of gold to be sold. They chose Abel R. Corbin, who had recently married Grant's younger sister. The Corbins lived in a fine five-story brownstone in Manhattan, and Gould and Fisk gained access to Grant through Corbin. The Grants were entertained at the theater and on the yacht of the speculators, who urged on the President the desirability for the country of raising the price of gold. Grant was noncommittal, but being seen publicly in their company gave these men a certain cachet.

In September 1869, Gould and Fisk began buying large amounts of gold and thereby driving up its price. If they were to succeed in their plan to corner the market, the Treasury had to lessen or totally suspend the sale of gold. Grant, about to leave Washington for a vacation in Bedford, Pennsylvania, wrote to Boutwell, telling him to continue the policy of selling gold. He entrusted this letter, however, to Corbin to deliver to the assistant treasurer in New York, who was to give it to Boutwell when the latter came to the city. Corbin apparently thought that the sealed envelope was an instruction to suspend the gold sale, and so advised Gould.

At the latter's request, Corbin wrote his brother-in-law a long letter giving ostensibly neutral reasons for suspending gold sales by the Treasury. He sent the letter by courier to the vacationing Grant. Grant read the letter after finishing a game of croquet and advised the courier that there would be no reply. The courier went to the nearest telegraph office and wrote out a message saying "Letter delivered all right." But the message transmitted was slightly but significantly altered: "Letter delivered. All right."

Encouraged by this misleading response, the conspirators continued to bid up the price of gold. The result was to dry up available foreign exchange and sharply diminish both imports and exports. Early in the day on Friday, September 24—Black Friday—the price of gold reached $150 on the New York market, with the conspirators purchasing each offer of the precious metal. Boutwell, after conferring with Grant, wired instructions to the assistant treasurer in New York to sell $4 million worth of gold. This news on the open wire dramatically pricked the gold bubble. Within minutes, the price dropped to $133. But the adverse consequences to the economy, particularly to agriculture, would be felt for a long time. And the Black Friday panic which resulted from these market manipulations did not reflect favorably on the new President.

Grant in no way cooperated with the conspirators, and had nothing to gain from their success. But his public appearances as guests of such people as Gould and Fisk gave the impression that they might be privy to the government's plans about gold sales. Grant was not the first and certainly not the last President to enjoy hobnobbing with very wealthy individuals, but he should have had the good judgment to avoid these particular men.

Grant's first venture into foreign affairs proved equally unsuccessful. Senior naval officers were anxious to get at least a coaling station somewhere in the Caribbean Sea. President Johnson urged the annexation of both the Dominican Republic and Haiti, but a resolution authorizing the annexation was decisively defeated in the House of Representatives in the waning days of his administration. Grant devoted considerable time and effort to work out an agreement with the rulers of the Dominican Republic providing for annexation of that nation and its admission as a state. But the treaty he submitted to the Senate to accomplish that purpose was defeated by a vote of 28 to 28, two-thirds majority being required for passage. Not only was the treaty defeated, but Grant earned the lasting hostility of the aging and imperious chairman of the Senate Foreign Relations Committee, Charles Sumner.

This contretemps over Santo Domingo also alienated other Republican senators, including Carl Schurz of Missouri. Schurz was a German immigrant who had come to this country with his new wife in 1852. This was a time of vastly increased immigration from the German states following the failed uprisings of 1848. Schurz was a political activist by nature and was an early and successful ethnic politician. After settling in Watertown, Wisconsin, he became active in Republican politics. Schurz was valuable to the party because he could speak to German-American gatherings in German as well as English. In 1860, he crisscrossed the country campaigning for Lincoln.

Grant was very sensitive to criticism, and as men like Sumner and Schurz deserted him, he fell back on the quite uncritical senators of his party who were bosses of political machines in their states: Roscoe Conkling in New York, Simon Cameron in Pennsylvania, Oliver Morton in Indiana. Men such as these would not harp on Grant's failings as long as he gave them ironclad control over the federal patronage in their states. And these alliances further antagonized the Reform, or Liberal, element in the Republican Party.

Following the great growth of the federal government during and after the Civil War there came a demand for reform of the civil service. While Andrew Johnson was President, the Radical Republicans championed this idea as a way of limiting Johnson's power to make appointments. But when their man Grant succeeded Johnson, Republicans began having second thoughts about the need for competitive examinations and the abandonment of a patronage system of appointments. Grant nonetheless urged Congress to create a Civil Service Commission which would promulgate rules and regulations to reform the Civil Service. Congress did enact such a law, but the outcome in the Senate was touch and go—a motion to kill the bill failed by only one vote.

Grant appointed George William Curtis, a longtime champion of civil service reform, to chair the Commission. It made its report a year later, saying that examinations should be required for promotion within a department, and political assessments on federal jobholders should be outlawed. Grant requested enabling legislation to give these rules the force of law, but Congress balked. It not only refused to enact such legislation but it let the appropriation for the Civil Service Commission lapse. Grant took this as a disapproval of reform by Congress and did not raise the matter again. Not until 1883, when Congress passed the Pendleton Act in the administration of Chester A. Arthur, would the first major step toward civil service reform take place.

Reformers of various sorts coalesced into a Liberal Republican movement during the latter part of Grant's first term. Alienated by Grant for a number of reasons, they formed a political organization in 1872. A Liberal state convention in Missouri under the leadership of Carl Schurz adopted a series of resolutions calling for "universal amnesty" (removal of political disabilities on ex-Confederates), a return to "local control" of government in the South, reduction of the tariff, and civil service reform. Those sympathetic to these proposals were urged to meet in Cincinnati on May 1, 1872. The convention which met in that city on that day was probably one of the most unusual in American political history. Grant's most recent biographer, Jean Edward Smith, describes the event in these words:

> ... the assemblage comprised a heterogeneous collection of free traders, disillusioned reformers, and civil libertarians, plus a considerable number of politicians who had lost factional struggles in the party and who expected to benefit from Grant's defeat. They were joined by a fluttering of East Coast intellectuals who had tired of cigar smoke in the White House: Edwin L. Godkin of *The Nation,* William Cullen Bryant of the *Evening Post,* James Russell Lowell and David A. Wells of the *North American Review,* and a covey of Adamses. The aim of the gathering, as Carl Schurz phrased it in his keynote address, was to elect an administration "which the best people of this country can be proud of."[3]

None of the delegates had been chosen by anyone but themselves, but the convention indulged in all of the backroom maneuvering typical of more orthodox political gatherings. It ended up nominating as its candidate for President Horace Greeley, the longtime editorial voice of their Republican Party as editor of the *New York Tribune.* His party credentials were impeccable, but he had oscillated back and forth on the major questions of the day and had championed some rather odd movements in his long career. No sooner had the convention done its work than some of its most prominent members threw up their hands in dismay:

> Godkin was astounded when he heard the news. "We suppose," he wrote in *The Nation,* "that a greater degree of incredulity and disappointment ... has not been felt ... since the news of the first battle of Bull Run." Bryant was

equally overwhelmed on learning of his old rival's triumph: "I should at any time beforehand have said that that thing was utterly impossible—that it could not be done by men in their senses," he wrote; "But bodies of men as individuals sometime lose their wits, and ... the average reason of a large assembly is sometimes sheer insanity."[4]

The Democratic National Convention met in Baltimore in July. Remembering how poorly the party had performed in the presidential election of 1868, the delegates swallowed their pride and endorsed Greeley. The sixty-one-year-old editor waged an active campaign, but in vain. He did not carry a single northern state, and his only electoral triumphs occurred in winning three southern states and three border states. The campaign also ended in personal tragedy. His invalid wife, Mary, died shortly before the election, and he himself died on November 29, 1872, three weeks after the election.

What the liberal Republicans and the Democrats had been unable to do to Grant and his Republican stalwarts in the election of 1872, a series of unfolding scandals and the Panic of 1873 bade fair to accomplish. The first of these scandals was the Crédit Mobilier affair, which broke just before the 1872 election. In no way did it implicate Grant, but it did implicate a number of prominent Republicans who had been members of the House of Representatives in 1868 and 1869 and were still active in politics.

In September 1872, two months before the election, the anti-administration *New York Sun* broke the Crédit Mobilier scandal. Its page-one story was headlined "The King of Frauds. How the Crédit Mobilier Bought Its Way Through Congress."

All but one of the accused were Republicans: Henry Wilson was the Republicans' vice presidential nominee; Schuyler Colfax was the sitting Vice President and previously had been Speaker of the House; George Boutwell had been Secretary of the Treasury. Congressman Oakes Ames of Massachusetts was charged with having given or sold at a discount to members of Congress stock in a corporation called Crédit Mobilier of America during the winter of 1867–1868.

The Crédit Mobilier was a Pennsylvania corporation owned by men who controlled the Union Pacific Railroad, one of them Ames. The Union Pacific contracted portions of the building and equipping of the railroad to Crédit Mobilier at highly inflated prices, which was good for Crédit Mobilier but bad for the Union Pacific. After the distribution of the stock, legislation favorable to the Union Pacific had passed both houses of Congress, first in 1868 and then in 1871.

The original account in the *Sun,* like many press reports, proved to contain major inaccuracies. But upon further sifting twelve congressman—eleven of them Republicans—were accused of having received Crédit Mobilier shares as a gift or at a discounted price. Two congressional committees investigated the matter at length and came to the remarkable conclusion that Ames had bribed members of Congress, but only one member—James Brooks of New York—was guilty of taking a bribe. The House, in a tumultuous session in March 1873, voted to censure Ames and Brooks, and let the matter drop there.

Several days later, on the day before it was to adjourn, Congress passed a resolution raising the salaries of its members from $5,000 per year to $7,500 and making the increase retroactive to the beginning of that Congress two years earlier. This measure was styled by its detractors as the "Salary Grab." Grant himself did not benefit from this law, but Republicans controlled both Houses of Congress, whose members did benefit. The considerable public outrage at the measure was directed largely at the Republican Party.

After the Civil War the nation went on a spree of railroad building. At the same time, Europe was enjoying a similar industrial expansion. Railroads require a tremendous investment of capital before they earn a cent of revenue. The necessary capital is raised by the sale of bonds, and many railroad bonds had been distributed in Europe—so many that the supply of European cash for additional purchase was greatly diminished.

Meanwhile, U.S. banks, exhilarated by the spending spree, were encouraged to lend money recklessly. An earlier-than-usual wheat crop in the summer of 1873 drew money away from the centers of capital. Banks were having difficulty marketing railroad acceptances, which were necessary for continued construction of rail lines. Depositors began to withdraw their money from banks. Jay Cooke & Company, a leading banking house which had almost single-handedly financed the Civil War for the Union, failed on September 18, and on September 20 the New York Stock Exchange simply closed for ten days. What had at first simply seemed a disaster for stock speculators soon became hard times for the nation as a whole, hard times which would last for several years.

> The Panic of 1873 revealed as nothing else could that Reconstruction had lost its primacy as the touchstone of party politics. American political life had been realigned. The political divide was no longer North versus South but East versus West, cities versus rural areas, and hard money—gold—versus soft money—greenbacks.[5]

At first, "soft money" and "hard money" advocates could be found in both major political parties but could gain ascendancy in neither. The Greenback and Populist Parties were both third parties committed to an inflationary money supply.[6]

When Congress convened in early 1875, both the House and the Senate agreed to pass a measure known as the Inflation Bill. It would markedly increase the amount of greenbacks in circulation to 400 million. The measure passed both houses by wide margins and was sent to the President for his signature. Grant considered it for a number of days, but finally—against the advice of a majority of his cabinet—vetoed it. He viewed it as the opening wedge in a congressional soft-money policy that would in the long run be very bad for the country. Administration forces in the Senate rallied enough votes to defeat a motion to override the veto; the motion carried by 34 to 30 but fell far short of the necessary two-thirds majority. The nation's financial community voiced its hearty approval of the veto, as did most of the eastern press.

SCANDAL AND HARD TIMES were a boon to the Democrats and a curse to the Republicans in the midterm elections of 1874. Normally Republican states such as Massachusetts, Wisconsin, and Michigan elected Democratic governors. The Republican majority of about a hundred in the House of Representatives turned into a Democratic majority of about two-thirds that amount. The Republicans held on to control of the Senate, but by a reduced margin. In May 1875, the Pennsylvania Republican Convention formally endorsed Grant for a third term as President. Grant quickly wrote the chairman of the state party, saying:

> I am not, nor have I ever been, a candidate for renomination. I would not accept a nomination if it were tendered, unless it should come under such circumstances as to make it an imperative duty—circumstances not likely to arise.[7]

During Grant's second term, scandals began to surface with what one writer has described as "clock-like regularity."

When Chief Justice Salmon P. Chase died in the spring of 1873, Grant nominated his Attorney General, George Williams of Oregon, to succeed Chase. Williams was scarcely an attorney of Supreme Court caliber, but the scrutiny which accompanied his nomination brought out improprieties in his conduct as Attorney General. He had paid personal expenses out of the contingency funds of the Department of Justice. Mrs. Williams had purchased the most expensive carriage in Washington and equipped it lavishly, all at government expense. Grant was forced to withdraw the nomination. He should have asked for Williams' resignation as Attorney General, but he did not.

Another scandal emerged in the Treasury Department in due course. For some time that department had paid informers who reported evasion of federal taxes, giving them half the amount collected from the delinquent taxpayer. The practice was obviously capable of abuse and was largely discontinued in 1872. But Congressman Benjamin "Spoons" Butler of Massachusetts inserted a rider to an appropriations bill which authorized its continuance in some cases.

The Secretary of the Treasury, William Richardson, who had succeeded George Boutwell, then entered into an agreement with Butler's friend John Sanborn, whereby Sanborn was authorized to collect delinquent taxes from entities such as railroads and distillers. Treasury officials told collectors *not* to pursue delinquent accounts so that Sanborn could go after them—and receive half of the amount collected. An investigation by the House Ways and Means Committee found that of the sum of more than $200,000 due Sanborn under the agreement, he had paid more than half that amount to unnamed "associates." No solid proof was brought forward to find that either

Richardson or Butler had personally benefited from Sanborn's activity, but there were surely grounds for suspicion. Sanborn's obdurate refusal to identify the unnamed associates stymied further investigation by the committee. Grant declined to call for Richardson's resignation, but the Secretary quit under a cloud in May 1874.

Next came Columbus Delano, who had succeeded his fellow Ohioan Jacob Cox as Secretary of the Interior. Department employees had been engaged in fraudulent land transactions, although there was no suggestion that the Secretary himself had profited from them. But he must have known of efforts by his son to obtain money from the Treasury by participating as a silent partner in companies hired by the department to survey federal lands. Young Delano was not only silent, but he apparently did no surveying. Secretary of State Fish urged Grant to ask for Delano's resignation, but Grant defended him, saying if he were to resign it would be an admission of guilt. But by midsummer of 1875, Delano himself finally realized that his usefulness was at an end and submitted his resignation.

Upon Richardson's resignation as Secretary of the Treasury in 1874, Grant appointed Benjamin Bristow of Kentucky to succeed him. Bristow had been the first person to hold the office of solicitor general in the Department of Justice, an office created at the same time as was the department itself in 1870. Before then, the Attorney General was a member of the President's cabinet but did not have a department of his own. After a stint as solicitor general, Bristow returned to the practice of law in Kentucky until the President called him back for the new assignment. Bristow brought both ability and a strong measure of somewhat rough-hewn ambition to the Treasury. He immediately reorganized the department to make it more businesslike, and less a haven for politically connected time-servers.

He then turned his attention to the notorious "Whiskey Ring." Producers and distributors of hard liquor were suspected of routinely bribing revenue agents to evade the stamp tax on distilled spirits. Investigators sent by Bristow audited outgoing shipments from cities such as St. Louis, Chicago, and Milwaukee, and confirmed to their satisfaction that such tax evasion was occurring. When Grant gave him the go-ahead, Bristow had Treasury agents descend on bottling plants in these and other cities, seize ledgers, books, and files, and impound tax receipts. Federal grand juries returned hundreds of indictments, and convictions followed. In St. Louis alone, evidence indicated that during the preceding two years more than $4 million in tax revenue had been evaded.

Both General John McDonald and John A. Joyce, collector and deputy collector in St. Louis, respectively, were indicted and convicted. Unfortunately for Grant, some of the evidence suggested that General Orville Babcock, principal secretary to the President, was also involved in the Ring. The evidence against him was circumstantial: he was a friend of McDonald's, he had visited St. Louis on occasion, and, most importantly, he had sent two cryptic telegrams to McDonald. They seemed to be in code, and were signed "Sylph." Bristow thought they were sent to keep McDonald apprised of the status of the impending seizures.

Babcock first asked for a military court of inquiry to clear his name. This seems to have been an odd request, since Babcock was acting in a civilian capacity as Grant's secretary. Grant approved, and a court-martial was convened. But prosecutors in St. Louis declined to surrender the files, took the case to a grand jury, and Babcock was indicted. Grant testified by deposition for his secretary, and Babcock was acquitted by a jury.

Babcock's acquittal meant that he would suffer no criminal punishment, but not that he was blameless or discreet. Courts rightly require the government to prove its case beyond a reasonable doubt when a crime is charged because of the severity of the punishment of imprisonment. But failure to adduce evidence meeting that high standard against Babcock in his criminal trial does not mean that one should approve or endorse his conduct or his judgment. Even Grant apparently realized this, because when Babcock returned from St. Louis, he was not restored to his secretarial position; he was instead given the post of inspector of lighthouses.

Early in 1876, William Belknap, another ex–Army general, who had succeeded Rawlins as Secretary of War, brought further criticism on the administration. His first wife, presumably with his connivance, had made a deal with the Army sutler at Fort Sill, a large post in Indian Territory, now Oklahoma. The understanding provided that in return for the lucrative job of feeding and supplying the troops stationed at the fort, the sutler would split his profits with her. When she died, Belknap married her younger sister, who continued the arrangement and proceeded to spend lavishly on clothing and personal effects. When this situation became public, Grant did demand and receive Belknap's resignation as Secretary of War.

GRANT WAS NOT an introspective man, and as he stood with Emperor Dom Pedro to start the steam engine at the Centennial Exhibition, it is doubtful that he thought about the successes and failures of his administration. He was already a lame duck, and it would be for history to judge him as a President. He had not been nearly as bad a President as various twentieth-century polls rating the occupants of that office would suggest. Out of seven polls described in Henry Abraham's recent book *Justice, Presidents, and Senators,* Grant is rated below all occupants of that office except Warren G. Harding in five of them. And in the other two he was rated as a "failure" along with seven others. But surely Grant's accomplishments exceed those of predecessors such as John Tyler and Millard Fillmore, neither of whom are rated as "failures" in these polls. The arbitration of the *Alabama* claims, the enactment of the Ku Klux Act, the veto of the Inflation Act, and the successful prosecution of the Whiskey Ring were all to his credit.

But his eight years in the White House had also been tainted by scandal, reaching into his official family if never implicating him personally. And scandals such as the Crédit Mobilier— which had no connection at all with Grant—had hurt the Republican Party. As federal troops were being withdrawn from the South, it became obvious that the former Confederate states would become a solid bloc of votes for the Democrats. The hard times brought on by the Panic of 1873 were sure to redound to the benefit of the party out of power. For the first time in twenty years, the Democratic Party in 1876 had at least an even chance of electing its candidate for President.

— CHAPTER 2 —

Rutherford Birchard Hayes was born on October 4, 1822, in Delaware, Ohio, a small town about thirty miles north of Columbus. His father and mother, Rutherford and Sophia Birchard Hayes, had migrated with their children Lorenzo and Sarah five years earlier to join other Vermonters who had settled in Delaware. Another daughter, Fanny, was born in 1820. But after Rutherford's birth, misfortune struck. First his sister Sarah and then his father died. Sophia Hayes was left a widow. She was no stranger to sorrow; her father, mother, and a brother and sister had died of typhus in Vermont before she was twenty-one.

Young Rutherford—called "Rud"—was a sickly child for the first two years of his life. He was very close to his sister Fanny, and his mother's younger brother, Sardis, who had emigrated with the family, took a fatherly interest in him. Rud attended local schools until age fifteen, when with Sardis's financial help he went east to attend Webb's Preparatory School in Middletown, Connecticut. A year later he entered Kenyon College, in Gambier, Ohio. He was required to pass examinations in Latin, Greek, mathematics, and grammar in order to be admitted. At the beginning and end of each term, he walked the forty-mile distance between Delaware and Gambier.

Rud had his share of run-ins with college authorities enforcing parietal rules but found the curriculum not overly demanding. He participated actively in the affairs of the Philomathesian Society, the college literary and debating organization. In his junior year he was elected treasurer of the society, and in his senior year he became president. His interest in politics quickened; in 1842 he journeyed to Dayton to hear a speech by Henry Clay, the Whig leader whom he greatly admired. In his senior year he buckled down to his studies—chemistry, mathematics, and "mental philosophy," and on his own read history and biography. He was rewarded by being named valedictorian and class speaker in 1842.

Throughout his life, Hayes demonstrated a capacity for making and keeping friends. Two of those closest to him at Kenyon were Stanley Matthews and Guy Bryan. Bryan was from Texas, a nephew of Stephen Austin, and would later fight in the Confederate Army while Hayes served in the Union Army. They corresponded regularly before and after the Civil War.

Matthews, a fellow Ohioan, would later become a principal adviser to Hayes during the presidential election of 1876. Hayes, in turn, nominated him to be a justice of the Supreme Court of the United States. For a small, isolated college, Kenyon produced a remarkable number of national political figures of this era. In addition to Hayes and Matthews, both Edwin M. Stanton, Lincoln's Secretary of War, and David Davis, whom Lincoln appointed to the Supreme Court of the United States, attended Kenyon.

After graduation, Hayes decided on a career in the law. As was common then, he began to read law in the office of a lawyer in Columbus. Fanny and her husband had moved there, which made it attractive to him as a place to study; but after nearly a year, he decided he was not progressing fast enough. He decided to attend Harvard Law School. He obtained some money from the sale of family land, and his uncle Sardis contributed the balance toward his expenses at Harvard.

He enrolled there in August 1843 and was very impressed with professors such as Joseph Story, a sitting justice of the U.S. Supreme Court, and Simon Greenleaf, who had written the authoritative *Treatise on the Law of Evidence.* Story at this time had served over thirty years on the Court, having been appointed an associate justice by James Madison in 1811. But he disappointed Madison and his predecessor, Thomas Jefferson, by quickly moving into the camp of Chief Justice John Marshall, who shared his preference for a strong federal government.

Story did not confine himself to judging and teaching. Like Greenleaf, he had written highly regarded texts on several branches of the law. In addition, he had been president of a bank in Salem, Massachusetts, written speeches for Daniel Webster, and drafted bills for Congress dealing with the federal judiciary. While Greenleaf concentrated on the subject matter of the course, Hayes found that Story tended to introduce extraneous anecdotes from his own experience.

Outside of class, he listened to the orations of historian George Bancroft and Congressman Robert Winthrop, as well as the speeches of septuagenarian John Quincy Adams. Adams, after serving as President, returned to the House of Representatives as a member from Massachusetts. Hayes found the orations of Daniel Webster, one of his Whig heroes, less impressive than he had imagined. All in all, 1844 was an exciting time to be in a city like Boston, where there was much agitation over proposals

Rutherford B. Hayes (seated, left), Guy Bryan (standing), and Stanley Matthews (seated, right), taken in either 1843 or 1848.

to annex Texas to the Union, and much interest in the presidential race between the Whig candidate, Henry Clay, and the Democrat, James Polk.

Hayes returned to Ohio for the summer of 1844 but went back to Harvard in the fall of that year to finish up his studies, which he did in January 1845. He was now twenty-two years old and ready to settle down to the practice of law.

In March he went to Marietta, Ohio, to be examined by a committee of lawyers for admission to the bar. He passed the examination and was admitted to practice, returning to Columbus by way of Cincinnati. Cincinnati was then by far the largest city in the state, with a population of nearly 50,000. Columbus had a population of only 6,000, and Fremont—where Sardis lived and where Hayes planned to practice—had barely 1,000 inhabitants. Hayes chose a small town on the advice of his Harvard teacher, Professor Greenleaf, who counseled against hanging out one's shingle in a large city.

Hayes' business in Fremont generally consisted of debt collections and the unscrambling of land titles. In the spring of 1846 the Mexican War began, and Hayes very nearly enlisted—but changed his mind at the last minute. He was critical of President Polk, but greatly admired General Zachary Taylor, who commanded American troops in their successful advance across the Rio Grande and into northern Mexico.

Ill with a throat ailment in the spring of 1847, Hayes took the summer off and traveled to the East Coast with John Pease, a Fremont businessman, cousin, and client. Such an absence did not bespeak a thriving law practice. In the fall of 1848, he again took an extended vacation with Sardis, this time by steamboat to New Orleans, then on to Galveston and the Texas Gulf Coast to visit his classmate Guy Bryan. Warmly received and lavishly entertained by Bryan and his fellow planters, Hayes was here exposed for the first time to the institution of slavery. He felt it was not only bad for the slaves, but bad for the masters. Returning to Ohio after four months, he wound up his practice in Fremont and moved to Cincinnati, now wanting to meet the challenge of a larger world.

He rented a room with another young lawyer, a room which served as both living quarters and office for both of them. Business was slow at first, but Hayes relished the flourishing social and intellectual life of Ohio's largest city. More importantly, he became engaged to Lucy Webb, the daughter of a friend of his mother's, in June 1851. Nine years his junior, Lucy had been too young to be thought of as a marriage prospect when they had first met in Columbus, but she was now twenty. After an engagement that lasted more than a year, they were married in December 1852.

Rutherford and Lucy Hayes began what would be a long and happy marriage by taking a short honeymoon trip to Columbus. Here Hayes argued his first case before the supreme court of Ohio. His client was James Summons, whom a jury had convicted of murdering two family members (he had poisoned four with arsenic but the other two had survived). Hayes argued on appeal that the testimony of a key witness had been improperly admitted. Shortly afterward he heard that a majority of the court favored reversal, but then later learned that one justice had changed his mind and the court was deadlocked. He would argue the case twice more, and finally, four years later, the supreme court upheld Summons' conviction.

The question before the court was whether an incriminating statement made by a witness at an earlier trial of Summons could be testified to by someone who had heard her at that trial; the witness had since died. At this time it was not customary to have verbatim transcripts of trial testimony where there had been no appeal, and so the state offered the testimony of one of the prosecutor's clerks at that trial who had written down what the witness said. Hayes had argued that such testimony violated the hearsay rule, but the supreme court decided by a vote of 3 to 1 that it was properly admitted under an exception to that rule. The Governor, however, commuted Summons' sentence to life in prison.

Hayes' reputation as a criminal defense lawyer grew with his performance in this and other capital cases. One such case was that of Nancy Farrer, charged with the murder of an eight-year-old boy. He argued that she was legally insane. The jury deliberated for days, and then brought in a verdict of guilty. Hayes appealed the conviction to the state supreme court, claiming that jury misconduct vitiated the verdict. The supreme court agreed and sent the case back for a new trial. This time Hayes persuaded the jury that Farrer was "of unsound mind"; she was saved from execution and was committed to a mental institution.

The publicity Hayes received in cases such as these was not bankable, and for more than a year after their marriage, the couple lived with Lucy's mother. But Hayes also developed a civil practice that was more remunerative than the criminal. His uncle Sardis had extensive real-estate holdings in and around Fremont, and was anxious to secure a rail line for the town. With its small population, Fremont could not be a destination, but it could be a way station on a railroad from Cleveland to Toledo. The Junction Railroad had been chartered to serve Fremont in that way, but then decided on a more direct route between Cleveland and Toledo which would bridge Sandusky Bay northeast of Fremont.

Hayes represented the Fremont interests and sought an injunction against the new route in federal court in Cincinnati. He argued that the new route would violate the company's charter—which called for it to go through Fremont—and also that a bridge across Sandusky Bay would be an obstruction to navigation. The case came before Justice John McLean in April 1853.

McLean was a justice of the Supreme Court of the United States, but at this time the justices also sat as trial judges in their respective geographic circuits.

McLean did issue an injunction, but only on the ground of violation of the charter, and not because of obstruction of navigation on Sandusky Bay. This left open to the railroad the option of merging with another line to avoid the charter problem, and it promptly did this. The new railroad offered to connect Fremont to Fort Wayne, Indiana, by a separate line, if the Fremont interests would drop the claim that the bridging of Sandusky Bay on the route between Cleveland and Toledo would obstruct navigation on the bay. Hayes advised his clients to accept the compromise, and they did.

That same year Lucy gave birth to the first of their seven sons—Birchard, called "Birch." The following year the couple felt able to buy a home of their own, and moved out of Mrs. Webb's house.

Hayes was active in local politics during this period, helping to start the fledgling Republican Party in Cincinnati. In December 1858, the city solicitor of Cincinnati was killed in a railroad accident, and Hayes was one of the lawyers nominated to fill the position. It was regarded as a political plum; the pay of $3,500 per year was more than twice that of a state trial judge. After thirteen ballots of the sharply divided city council, Hayes was chosen.

One of Hayes' rivals for the position wrote of the winner's "luck" in obtaining the position. But as Hayes' most recent biographer, Ari Hoogenboom, points out:

> In time, Hayes' luck became an axiom for Ohio political pundits, but it was neither blind nor dumb. Hayes never appeared to be seeking office, but by instinctively and deliberately enhancing his availability, he created conditions con-

ducive to good luck. Eschewing extreme positions, he made himself acceptable to a wide spectrum of voters. Genuinely decent and kind, he was careful not to take his friends for granted nor to offend his rivals. . . . His reputation for fairness and integrity made Hayes acceptable to many with whom he was not in agreement.[1]

Hayes would enthusiastically support Abraham Lincoln when he received the Republican nomination for President in 1860. In February, the President-elect left his home in Springfield, Illinois, on a railroad journey which would take him through Indiana, Ohio, Pennsylvania, New York, New Jersey, and Maryland, and ultimately to Washington, D.C. Hayes met the train in Indiana and rode with the presidential party to Cincinnati.

His admiration for Lincoln deepened, but his worry about the fate of the Union increased. No sooner had Lincoln been elected in November than South Carolina began a procession among the states of the lower South to secede from the Union. James Buchanan was a lame-duck President until March 4, and he simply threw up his hands at the situation confronting him. Lincoln, succeeding Buchanan, debated with his cabinet for six weeks over what to do about the Union garrison at Fort Sumter, located on an island in the harbor of Charleston, South Carolina. The Confederates demanded that the Union troops surrender; finally, on April 12, the shore batteries in Charleston Harbor opened fire, and the Union garrison evacuated the fort two days later.

Hayes responded with alacrity to Lincoln's call for volunteers. There was none of the ambivalent attitude that he had felt about enlisting in the Mexican War. Hayes and his Kenyon friend, Stanley Matthews, volunteered together, and in the first week of June, Hayes was appointed a major and Matthews a lieutenant colonel in the Twenty-third Regiment of Ohio Volunteers. Hayes would fight for the Union until mustered out four years later.

The regiment was billeted at newly established Camp Chase on the outskirts of Columbus from early June until late July. Hayes, who had no previous military experience, took readily to his new role, learning quickly about the three ways to do things: the right way, the wrong way, and the Army way. When the colonel in command, William S. Rosecrans, was absent, Matthews and Hayes were in charge. " 'What we don't know, we guess at,' Hayes reported. 'And you may be sure that we are kept busy guessing.' He enjoyed it all 'as much as a boy does a Fourth of July.' "[2]

Rosecrans was promoted to brigadier general and ordered into then western Virginia—now the state of West Virginia. In late July, the Twenty-third Regiment was ordered to join Rosecrans's forces at Clarksburg. Thus began a campaign of several months to drive the Confederates out of West Virginia. Hayes came under fire for the first time at Carnifex Ferry on the Gauley River and was pleased with his coolness. In October the regiment went into winter quarters at Fayetteville, and Hayes was promoted to lieutenant colonel. There being not much to do, he boned up on military texts and enjoyed life in the outdoors. In February he obtained leave to visit Lucy and their newborn son, Joseph, who lived only eighteen months.

After inconclusive and desultory fighting in the spring of 1862 in West Virginia, Hayes' regiment, along with five others in the division of General Jacob Cox, was pulled out of West Virginia and assigned to General Jesse Reno's corps of Ambrose Burnside's army. Burnside's corps was part of General George McClellan's Army of the Potomac, which was now pursuing the

Confederate force of General Robert E. Lee. Lee had crossed the Potomac after the Second Battle of Manassas and was marching through Maryland.

The Union Army marched north to Frederick, Maryland, and then turned west into the Blue Ridge Mountains. One of Lee's aides had left behind a paper, found by a Union officer, which showed that Lee's troops were badly divided. McClellan sought to push through Turner's Gap in South Mountain, and ordered Reno's corps to do it; Reno in turn chose Cox's division and it fell to Hayes and the Ohio Twenty-third Regiment to spearhead the attack. Hayes led his men up a mountain path toward the pass, where they were met by a strong Confederate force. Hayes twice ordered the troops to charge, and finally the enemy broke. Just as they did, Hayes was hit by a musket ball in his right arm, fracturing the bone and leaving a large hole.

At first he tried to continue directing his men, but he felt faint and had to lie down. Weak from the loss of blood, he was only intermittently conscious and was briefly left in front of his own lines at the mercy of the Confederates. But one of his lieutenants rescued him, and he was taken to a field hospital where his wound was dressed, and then to the rear by ambulance. A local merchant in Middletown, Maryland, took Hayes into his house to recuperate from the wound. The next day he sent telegrams to Lucy and others telling of his wound.

Unfortunately, due to a mix-up, Lucy did not receive the telegram, and learned of Hayes' wound only from a second telegram received several days later. The message appeared to have come from Washington, and Lucy started for that city with Will Platt, Hayes' brother-in-law. But after a search at military hospitals in the capital proved unsuccessful, they discovered that the telegram had come not from Washington, but from Middletown. They took the train to Frederick and located Hayes in the merchant's home. Hayes now improved steadily, but the arm continued to give him spells of pain.

He went on leave in October and November 1862, brushed off an offer to support him for election to Congress, and returned to the Army. He was in West Virginia for a time but finished the war in the thick of the fighting in the Valley of Virginia in the summer and fall of 1864. He was promoted to brigadier general and was mustered out of the Army in 1865.

Being a warrior had been hard, but it had given Hayes the experience of a lifetime. When his soldiers were leaving for home, Hayes doubted "that many of them will ever see as happy times again as they have had in the Army." As he was about to lose the camaraderie of camp and field, he realized that the four most glorious years of his life were ending. But, if war had been fascinating, he sensed that peace could be enchanting and knew that its time had come. To his mother, Hayes simply wrote, "I am very happy to be through with the war."[3]

Even though he had declined to run in 1862, Hayes was elected to Congress from his Cincinnati district in 1864 while still in the Army. The first session of that Congress did not begin until December 1865. Hayes left for Washington in late November by himself. There had, of course, been no representatives from any of the seceded states during the war, and now the Ohio Republican delegation voted to oppose any representation from those states for the time being. This Congress would be the first to deal with the political aftermath of the war, and one of the first orders of business would be to decide how the states of the former Confederacy should be integrated back into the Union.

Lincoln had favored a conciliatory policy toward these states.

In 1864 he had proposed that Louisiana—by that time wholly under the control of the Union military—should be "readmitted" when 10 percent of the 1860 voting population took an oath of loyalty to the Union. The Radical wing of the Republican Party—headed by Benjamin Wade of Ohio and Charles Sumner of Massachusetts in the Senate, and by Thaddeus Stevens of Pennsylvania in the House, favored something closer to a "Carthaginian Peace": these states should be treated for the present as "conquered provinces" rather than as sister states.

There was also disagreement as to which branch of the government should have the lead role in this reconstruction of the seceded states. In the summer of 1864, Lincoln had killed by pocket veto the Wade-Davis Bill, which would have asserted congressional authority in this area. He felt that he might have more constitutional authority under his powers as Commander in Chief than Congress did under its enumerated powers. When Andrew Johnson succeeded Lincoln in April 1865, the new President's expressed views on the subject seemed acceptable to the Radicals, but the passage of time revealed an ever-deepening rift. Johnson, a Tenneseean, had been one of the few southern Democrats to support the Union war effort and the Thirteenth Amendment to the Constitution, which outlawed slavery. But beyond this he was a states' rights Democrat, agreeing in principle with a maxim of the Democratic Party: "The Union as it was, the Constitution as it is."

When the full Republican caucus met, it agreed with Stevens' proposal to create a joint committee of the House and Senate on Reconstruction to deal with the revival of representation for the former Confederate states. No new legislators from these states would be recognized until Congress decided to recognize them. Hayes was fully in accord with these views. He wrote to Lucy that the Republican leadership in the House consisted of

Stevens, William Kelley of Pennsylvania, and Roscoe Conkling of New York. He was reunited in Washington with his Kenyon College friend Rowland Trowbridge, now a congressman from Michigan.

As a very junior member of the House, he could not expect important committee assignments, and his expectations were not disappointed. He was assigned to the Land Claims Committee, and he became chairman of the Joint House and Senate Committee on the Library. Literate as he was, he enjoyed this undemanding chairmanship.

A good deal of the House members' energy was devoted to the drafting of a fourteenth amendment to the Constitution, which would prohibit any state from denying to any person the equal protection of the laws, and from depriving any person of life, liberty, or property without due process of law. Much of the debate centered around disenfranchisement of former Confederate officials and around devising a remedy if a state should deny the vote to persons because of race or color.

The Republican-dominated Congress decided to make ratification of the Fourteenth Amendment a condition of the readmission of the seceded states. The Republicans were convinced that if there were no constitutional protection for the newly freed slaves, the governments of the former Confederate states would be controlled by the same white oligarchy responsible for secession—with dire consequences for the former slaves. But there was also a less altruistic motive in the Republican view: unless the freed men were allowed to vote, these states would be solidly Democratic on election day. Southern whites regarded both the Civil War and the Reconstruction which followed it as Republican-inspired, and would not soon forget either of these events.

President Johnson opposed making the ratification of the

Fourteenth Amendment a condition of readmission, and the gulf between him and the congressional Republicans became wider. Johnson also vetoed a reauthorization of the Freedmen's Bureau, an agency designated to operate in the South to help the freed slaves. Hayes was ambivalent about this measure, feeling that there was some truth in Democratic charges of corruption in the bureau. But otherwise he sided with the radicals to override the President's veto of the Civil Rights Act of 1866, a statutory forerunner of the Fourteenth Amendment.

Hayes was easily reelected from his district in October 1866, and in December he returned to Washington with Lucy and his third son, Rutherford Jr., known as "Rud," just as his father had been. The Radical wing of the Republican Party had greatly increased its strength in Congress in the election of 1866 and veered closer to a collision with the President. In the spring of 1867 Congress passed, over Johnson's vetoes, a series of Reconstruction Acts which in effect imposed military government on the unreconstructed states in the South.

Early in 1867, Jacob Cox—Hayes' commanding general at South Mountain—decided not to run for reelection as Governor of Ohio. William Henry Smith, Ohio Secretary of State, urged Hayes to run, but at first he demurred. Some of his backers used the time-honored claim that only he could carry the state ticket to victory, and he finally agreed to be a candidate. At the state convention in June he was supported by the Radical wing of the party led by Senator Wade and was opposed by supporters of Salmon P. Chase, now Chief Justice of the United States. He resigned from Congress in August, effective in October. His first foray into national political life had been competent but unspectacular.

He viewed the gubernatorial campaign as an opportunity to urge approval of a referendum measure which would allow blacks to vote in Ohio. Many Ohioans who favored the Union cause in the Civil War and emancipation of the slaves in the southern states drew back at the idea of political, to say nothing of social, equality in Ohio. Hayes also was not above "waving the bloody shirt" and denouncing the leading Democrats—including his opponent, Allen G. Thurman—as onetime supporters of secession.

Hayes won a narrow victory in October 1867, garnering a margin of less than 3,000 votes out of nearly half a million cast. The referendum allowing black suffrage failed. The Democrats gained control of the legislature and voted to rescind Ohio's ratification of the Fourteenth Amendment. The amendment was nonetheless proclaimed as law by Secretary of State William H. Seward in the following year.

The Governor of Ohio had no veto power, and so Hayes was an outsider in the state legislative process. But members of the Ohio congressional delegation on occasion consulted him about public opinion in the state. Queried as to what Ohioans wanted in the impeachment trial of Andrew Johnson, Hayes responded "conviction," without referring to any opinion poll.

Hayes led the Ohio delegation to the Republican convention in Chicago in May 1868, held shortly after Johnson's acquittal by a one-vote margin in the Senate. He was pleased with the nomination of Grant as the party's candidate for President, but disappointed that his fellow Ohioan, Ben Wade, lost out to Schuyler Colfax of Indiana for the vice presidential candidacy. Grant handily carried Ohio in the November election.

The state Republican convention nominated Hayes for his second term as Governor by acclamation in June 1869, and he again campaigned for equal rights for men of all races. The Democrats, on the other hand, opposed ratification of the Fifteenth Amendment, which would prohibit denial of the right to vote because of race. They nominated George Hunt Pendleton, who had been the Democratic vice presidential candidate in the election of 1864. Pendleton championed a "soft money" policy, urging that the government's Civil War debts be paid in depreciated greenbacks. The election in October was another close one, with the result not known until the following day. This time Hayes won by more than 7,000 votes, and the Republicans narrowly gained control of the state legislature.

Hayes liked being Governor. The office required little heavy lifting of any kind, and he loved the state of Ohio. He and his family moved into the former home of Noah H. Swayne, now a member of the Supreme Court of the United States. It was larger than their previous quarters, and the rent was reasonable. During his second term, Ohio ratified the Fifteenth Amendment and in response to Hayes' pleas established the institution which would later become Ohio State University. When the legislature was not in session, Hayes traveled about Ohio and on one occasion to Washington, where he visited with President Grant. Grant extolled the need to annex the Dominican Republic, but Hayes remained unconvinced.

Hayes did not seek a third term as Governor, and retired to private life in January 1872. He and Lucy rented rooms in a hotel in Cincinnati for themselves and their two youngest children—Fanny, now four, and Scott, aged two. He dabbled in railroad promotions and land speculation, and continued to support Republican causes. The party suffered defeat in the election of 1873, partly because of the Panic, and partly because of the Crédit Mobilier and Salary Grab scandals, Hayes thought.

In the next year Sardis Birchard, who had been a substitute father as well as an uncle to Hayes, died. Birch and Webb, Hayes' two oldest boys, were both attending Cornell University in Ithaca, New York. Manning, the youngest child, took sick and died shortly after his first birthday. Hayes campaigned for Ohio Congressman Charles Foster from his district, who was reelected in spite of Democratic successes nationwide in 1874. He and Lucy now moved from Cincinnati to Spiegel Grove, a house built for them by Sardis in Fremont.

Hayes' stint in private life was short; the Republican Party turned to him again in March 1875 and urged him to run for Governor for the third time. He was at first loath to do so—Alphonso Taft from Cincinnati very much wanted the nomination. But this time the governorship had an added appeal for Hayes; if elected, he would surely be "mentioned" as a potential Republican presidential nominee in 1876. Grant's disclaimer of interest in a third term had an escape clause to it, but any doubt was put to rest by the House of Representatives, controlled as it was by Democrats, adopting a resolution declaring that any breach of the "no third term" tradition established by George Washington would be "fraught with peril to our free institutions." The Republican convention then would be, for the first time since 1860, a genuinely open one, with no odds-on favorite. As an experienced Governor of a crucial state, Hayes would be bound to be a factor in the contest.

He was concerned about the small salary paid the Governor, but eventually gave his supporters the green light. At the state convention in June 1875, he defeated Taft by a margin of more than two to one. He campaigned diligently but with less enthusiasm than in the past. Hard times produced by the Panic of 1873, which had given the Democrats a national success in the 1874 congressional elections, still persisted. But the usual Hayes "luck" prevailed, and he defeated the incumbent Democrat, William Allen, by a margin of 5,000 votes in October 1875.

Hayes was inaugurated in January 1876 and went about performing the now familiar duties of that office. But almost immediately attention focused on him as a possible presidential candidate in the November election. Senator John Sherman in January urged his fellow Ohio Republicans to send a delegation to the national convention solidly committed to Hayes. The Governor had several years earlier refused to allow his name to be placed before the legislature as a candidate for senator in opposition to Sherman, and he now reaped the rewards of his instinctive good judgment at that time. At the state convention in April, the delegates voted unanimously to support Hayes for the party's presidential nomination.

Hayes would have a number of rivals for that nomination, several better known to the party and to the country as a whole. First and foremost was Representative James G. Blaine of Maine. Born in Pennsylvania, and educated there, he moved to Maine when in his twenties after he purchased an interest in a newspaper in Augusta. He left publishing after a few years to devote his full time to politics. He had the look and bearing of a statesman and was regarded as probably the best political orator of his day. Elected to the state legislature in 1858, he went to the U.S. House of Representatives in 1863. After only three terms in that body, he was elected Speaker, an office which at that time gave its holder a good deal more authority than it does now. Blaine held this office until the Democrats gained control of the House in 1875. In July 1876, he would be elevated to the Senate to fill a vacancy created by the appointment of Senator Lot Morrill to Grant's cabinet.

In Congress, Blaine walked a fine line, supporting much but not all of the legislative programs of the Radical Republicans. He made many friends in Congress, but he also had one bitter enemy—Roscoe Conkling, first a representative and then a senator from New York. The two men became the respective leaders of the Grant and anti-Grant factions within the Republican Party: Conkling led the "Stalwarts" favoring a third term for Grant, and Blaine led the "Half Breeds" in opposition to the President. Both would be seeking the Republican presidential nomination in 1876.

Blaine was falsely accused of participation in the Crédit Mobilier scandal, but he had a scandal of his own to explain. An investigating committee of the Democrat-controlled House accused him of having saved a land grant for the Little Rock & Fort Smith Railroad when he was Speaker of the House. In return, he requested and received from the railroad the privilege of selling bonds of the company on a very generous commission basis. Evidence of the truth or falsity of the charges was thought to rest in a collection known as the Mulligan Letters. Blaine obtained the letters from Mulligan but refused to turn them over to the committee. Instead, he read selected passages from the letters on the House floor, in a dramatic speech which satisfied his admirers but left a permanent cloud on his reputation.

Conkling was the undisputed Republican boss of New York State. He was elected to Congress in 1858 and to the Senate in 1867. He was a tall and impressive figure, thought to be overbearing by his detractors. Blaine, in a memorable jibe at him when they were both members of the House, decried his "haughty disdain, his grandiloquent swell, his majestic supereminent, overbearing, turkey-gobbler strut."[4] Conkling, noted for his vanity, would not forget those words.

Benjamin Bristow, who served in Grant's cabinet as Secretary of the Treasury, was also mentioned as a candidate. He was a favorite of the Reform element in the party, and no one doubted his ability. It was demonstrated by his detection, prosecution, and conviction of the Whiskey Ring described in the preceding chapter. But Grant felt that Bristow had unnecessarily brought about the prosecution of his private secretary, Orville Babcock, and he welcomed if he did not force Bristow's resignation from his cabinet. Grant himself would not be a candidate in 1876, but his unyielding opposition to Bristow prevented the latter from gaining any convention votes from the Stalwart wing of the party.

Oliver Perry Morton of Indiana was the favorite of the Radical Republicans. He had gone to work at age fifteen, first as apprentice to a druggist, and then as apprentice to a hatter. Dissatisfied with this life, he entered Miami University of Ohio and studied there for two years, becoming recognized as a skilled debater. He left college to read law in Centerville, Indiana, and eventually established a successful law practice in Wayne County in that state. He was one of the first to join the newly formed Republican Party in Indiana, and was the party's unsuccessful candidate for Governor in 1856. He became Indiana's wartime Governor, and was recognized as one of the ablest of the northern Republican executives. He fought a protracted battle with the Democratic state legislature, financing out of his own pocket the necessary expenses of the state government when the legislature refused to appropriate funds for that purpose.

Morton was crippled by a paralytic stroke in 1865 but lost none of his zest for politics. He was elected to the Senate in 1867, where he served until his death in 1877. He was one of the most fervent supporters of the radical reconstruction program in Congress. Just because he was so clearly identified with that wing of the party, and because he showed no enthusiasm for "reform," he had disadvantages as a candidate for the presidential nomination: "To the end of his life he was a power to be reckoned with in American politics, loved and honored by his friends, cordially hated by his enemies, and almost never ignored."[5]

The sixth aspirant for the nomination was John Hartranft, Governor of Pennsylvania. Like Hayes, he came from a populous state, and like Hayes, he had also served with distinction in the Union Army during the Civil War. But he was no better known nationally than Hayes, and less "available" than Hayes because Pennsylvania was likely to vote Republican whoever the party's candidate was; Ohio was a more doubtful state, which its Governor might carry but which another nominee might not.

Rutherford Hayes was assuredly not the favorite among these six aspirants for the Republican nomination; Blaine held that position. But Hayes had the unique distinction among this sextet of being the Governor of a swing state and of being acceptable to all factions of the party, even though he was the first choice of only a small minority. If the better-known candidates faltered, he could be a compromise choice.

The Republican National Convention met in Cincinnati on June 14. Such quadrennial conventions today generally do no more than confirm the results already reached in state-by-state primary elections held during the spring. But primaries were unknown in 1876. State delegates were chosen in state conventions, and these conventions had given Blaine more delegates than any of his rivals, but not enough to win the nomination on the first ballot.

Blaine had suffered a psychological blow to his candidacy the preceding Sunday, when ascending the steps of his church in Washington he collapsed and fell unconscious into the arms of his wife. He remained in that state for two days, but revived on the day before the convention opened and wired his managers in Cincinnati that he was on his way to complete recovery.

The convention was called to order on Wednesday in Exposition Hall, a huge wooden structure with twin towers, described by one observer as an "ambitious and disappointed railroad depot." Following the keynote speech and speeches devoted to proposed resolutions and the adoption of the party platform, the convention proceeded to the nominating speeches for the candidates on the afternoon of June 15. Sixteen speakers took the rostrum to nominate or second the nomination of no fewer than seven candidates. The most dramatic moment in this process was the speech by Colonel Robert Ingersoll nominating Blaine. A splendid orator at a time when oratory was valued far more than it is now, his speech concluded:

"Like an armed warrior, like a plumed knight, James G. Blaine marched down the halls of the American congress and threw his shining lance full and fair against the brazen forehead of every traitor to his country and every maligner of his fair reputation. For the Republican party to desert that gallant man now is as though an army should desert their general upon the field of battle. James G. Blaine is now and has been for years the bearer of the sacred standard of the Republican party. I call it sacred, because no human being can stand beneath its folds without becoming and without remaining free.

"Gentlemen of the Convention: In the name of the great republic, the only republic that ever existed upon the face of the earth; in the name of all her defenders and of all her supporters; in the name of all her soldiers living; in the name of her soldiers that died upon the field of battle; and in the name of those that perished in the skeleton clutch of famine at Andersonville and Libby, whose sufferings he so vividly remembers,—Illinois—Illinois nominates for the next president of this country that prince of parliamentarians, that leader of leaders James G. Blaine."[6]

The *Chicago Times* reported the speech in these words:

Ingersoll moved out from the obscure corner and advanced to the central stage. As he walked forward the thundering cheers, sustained and swelling, never ceased. As he reached the platform they took on an increased volume of sound, and for ten minutes the surging fury of acclamation, the wild waving of hats and handkerchiefs, transformed the scene from one of deliberation to that of a bedlam of rapturous delirium. Ingersoll waited with unimpaired serenity, until he should get a chance to be heard. . . . And then began an appeal, impassioned, artful, brilliant, and persuasive. . . . Possessed of a fine figure, a face of winning, cordial frankness, Ingersoll had half won his audience before he spoke a word. It is the attestation of every man that heard him, that so brilliant a master stroke was never uttered before a political Convention. Its effect was indescribable. The coolest-headed in the hall were stirred to the wildest expression. The adversaries of Blaine, as well as his friends, listened with unswerving, absorbed attention. Curtis sat spell-bound, his eyes and mouth wide open, his figure moving in unison to the tremendous periods that fell in a measured, exquisitely graduated flow from the Illinoisan's smiling lips. The matchless method and manner of the man can never be imagined from the report in type. To realize the prodigious force, the inexpressible power, the irrestrainable fervor of the audience requires actual sight.[7]

It was after five o'clock in the afternoon when all of the speeches were finished. Fearful that Ingersoll's nomination speech would lead to an early victory for Blaine if the votes were begun at once, his opponents obtained an adjournment to the following day. When they convened then, the first ballot gave Blaine a substantial lead. Three hundred seventy-nine votes were necessary for the nomination, and he received 285. Morton received 125, Bristow 113, Conkling 99, Hayes 61, and Hartranft 58. After four ballots, Blaine had gained only 7 votes, but after two more, his total had risen to 308. But Hayes' total had also risen, to 104. The seventh ballot was decisive. Indiana withdrew its votes for Morton, and gave most of them to Hayes. Kentucky withdrew Bristow's name and gave most of its votes to Hayes. When the clerk reached the State of New York on the roll call, Roscoe Conkling exacted his revenge for Blaine's allusion to his "turkey-gobbler strut." Sixty-one of the state's 70 votes now went to Hayes. At the end of the seventh ballot Hayes was the victor with 384 votes.

"My hand is sore with shaking hands," Hayes wrote to Birch at 6 p.m. Blaine graciously congratulated Hayes, who responded with equal graciousness. Hayes was momentarily overcome with emotion when he thought of how proud Uncle Sardis and his sister Fanny would have been, but on the whole he remained "calm and self-possessed."[8]

— CHAPTER 3 —

Samuel Jones Tilden

O<small>N</small> F<small>EBRUARY</small> 9, 1814, Samuel Jones Tilden was born in New Lebanon, New York, an upstate hamlet on the turnpike route between Albany and Pittsfield, Massachusetts. That route eventually became U.S. Highway 20, and New Lebanon today remains a village located just west of the New York–Massachusetts state line.

The Tilden family emigrated from England in the first part of the seventeenth century, settling first in Massachusetts, then moving to Connecticut, and finally to Columbia County, New York. Elam, Samuel's father, was a successful farmer and then the owner of a general store. As a sideline, he sold medicinal herbs on consignment from a nearby Shaker settlement. He and his wife, Polly, endured the usual sorrows and hardships of rural life at this time—crop failures, hard times, and the deaths of five of their children.

Samuel grew up into an abnormally delicate youth. He was zealously guarded against exposure of all kinds, padded with heavy clothing, warned against wet feet, and confined a great deal of the time within the house. . . . Thus coddled and impressed with his own frailty, it would have been surprising if the lad had not conceived an exaggerated impression of the gravity of his ailments. His early life seems to have been a succession of colds, fevers, and stomach troubles, and his earliest notes are crammed with recipes for remedies, long accounts of afflictions of his throat, lungs, teeth and stomach, and detailed descriptions of treatments to relieve pain. . . .[1]

What he missed in the companionship of outdoor activities with friends his own age he made up for by reading avidly and participating in the society of his elders. Samuel read books well beyond his age level, and while he was still young, his father came to defer to his judgment on political questions. At the age of sixteen Tilden was driven by his father to Williamstown, Massachusetts, to attend a preparatory school associated with Williams College. After spending only one term there, he returned to his family in New Lebanon where he acted as secretary for the local debating society. But his many illnesses and his bookishness as a youth were to leave a lasting impact on his character as a man. His biographer, A. C. Flick, observes:

Samuel J. Tilden missed the best experiences of childhood. Those golden hours with their spontaneous laughter, their joyous and winning irresponsibility, their romantic dreaming and robustious gusto were, unhappily, never a part of his life. His importunate mind leaped the span of childhood, and in so doing deprived his character of those qualities which would have mellowed and completed it; and there perished in those days the capacity for friendship, the experience of shared adventure which is the basis of trust, and—

Samuel Tilden, not dated.

most tragic of all—the free spirit of fun which would have made his character more responsive and his personality more likeable.[2]

In 1832 Tilden journeyed to New York City to continue his studies. He boarded with his mother's sister and roomed with his uncle, the Reverend Henry Davis Ware. His "studies" were an unsystematic hodgepodge, and his relations with his aunt proved unpleasant. He returned to New Lebanon after a few months and took an active part in the state and national elections of 1832. He wrote campaign manifestos for the Democratic state ticket headed by William Marcy for Governor.

Marcy was a member of the Albany Regency, one of the first political machines in the nation. It was led by Martin Van Buren, who would eventually become the eighth President of the United States. One of Van Buren's favorite places for relaxation was Lebanon Springs, a spa close to the Tildens' home. Elam Tilden's political advice was sought by both Van Buren and his friend Silas Wright. Samuel, with his keen interest in politics, surely overheard if he did not actually sit in on some of these conferences. As Tilden grew to maturity, Van Buren became one of his mentors.

Van Buren was born into an established Dutch family in the Hudson River valley town of Kinderhook in 1782. His formal education consisted of a few years in the village school. He became active in politics when only eighteen, following in his father's footsteps as a Jeffersonian Republican. Admitted to the New York Bar after working in a law office in New York City, in 1803 he moved back to Kinderhook to hang out his shingle. He climbed the ladder of New York politics rapidly, starting as county surrogate in 1808. Four years later, he was elected to the State Senate, where he adroitly shifted sides between the Republican factions in the state. He headed the "Bucktail" wing of his party, which opposed Governor DeWitt Clinton.

In 1821 the Bucktails elected Van Buren to the United States Senate, and in 1822 he was elected Governor. Van Buren's Albany Regency now controlled the state. Associated with him were Silas Wright, William L. Marcy, and Azariah Flagg. The

"Little Magician," as Van Buren was called by his supporters, would go on to become Governor of New York in 1828, an office which he resigned the following year to become Secretary of State in the administration of Andrew Jackson. He was a champion of the "spoils system," a term derived from his colleague Marcy's maxim that "to the victor belongs the spoils." This principle applied to politics meant that a newly elected administration should feel free to replace government employees from the previous one with its own party faithful. Van Buren suited action to words by securing the removal of more than one hundred postmasters in New York alone.

Van Buren and Vice President John C. Calhoun were both ambitious to succeed Jackson. Jackson ultimately chose Van Buren and placed him on the Democratic ticket in 1832 as the party's candidate for Vice President. The Democratic Party was victorious both in New York and the nation in 1832, reelecting Jackson President and electing Marcy Governor.

Tilden now returned to New York City, where he combined his elusive "studies" with writing pamphlets defending Jackson and Van Buren against their detractors. In June 1834 he entered Yale College in New Haven as a freshman, still supported by his family. But he stayed only one term, again returning to New Lebanon, where he was once more active in state politics. In 1835—the year of his majority—he returned to New York City and enrolled at New York University. His attendance at college was sporadic, but the bustling activity and cultural life of the city intrigued him. In 1836 he rejoiced in the election of the Tilden family friend Van Buren as President.

He continued his studies at New York University but abandoned them short of graduation. He then began the study of law in 1837, but due to his usual procrastination was not admitted to practice in the state until 1841. One of the reasons for this delay was that he took time off from his legal studies in 1840 to work for the reelection of Martin Van Buren, who faced an uphill battle.

Shortly before he retired from office in 1837, President Jackson had issued his Specie Circular, which required that payments for the purchase of government lands be made in gold or silver rather than in paper money. Jackson had issued the circular to dampen the often wild speculation in western lands, but it did more than that. British banks had demanded gold and silver from their correspondent American banks, while the price of cotton, on which the southern economy depended, declined. Only a few days after Van Buren's inauguration in March 1837, several of the cotton brokerage houses in New Orleans failed, and the panic soon spread to the New York City banks. The ensuing hard times would hover like a dark cloud over the administration of the new President.

The country was on the mend by 1840, but the opposition had now coalesced into the Whig Party, and that party decided to take a new electoral tack. In 1836 the Whigs had been so divided that they ran regional presidential candidates in different parts of the country, including Henry Clay and William Henry Harrison. They were defeated by Van Buren.

Clay, Harrison, and Daniel Webster were the most prominent figures in the Whig leadership. Clay had lost to Jackson in 1832, and to Van Buren in 1836. With the Whigs smelling victory as the election of 1840 drew near, Clay very much desired the nomination again. He was certainly their ablest candidate, but he had lost twice, and this was enough to cause the Whig managers to turn elsewhere. They held their convention in Harrisburg, Pennsylvania, in December 1839, a remarkably early date. They nominated William Henry Harrison as their candidate, and John Tyler of Virginia as his running mate.

Harrison, at least on paper, seemed a strange choice. If successful, he would be sixty-eight at the time of his inauguration in 1841. He had been born to the Virginia aristocracy just before the beginning of the Revolutionary War and enlisted in the Army at the age of eighteen, becoming an aide to "Mad Anthony" Wayne at the Battle of Fallen Timbers in what was then the Northwest Territory. After leaving the Army, he had been appointed Governor of Indiana Territory, a post which he held for more than ten years.

There was at this time a gathering confederacy of Indians under the leadership of Shawnee Chief Tecumseh, and Harrison led a force of Kentucky and Indiana militia against them at the Battle of Tippecanoe in 1811. Two years later, during the War of 1812, he commanded an American force against the British and Canadians at the Battle of the Thames in Ontario. He was victorious; the battle ended with the death of Tecumseh and the flight of the British commander.

In retrospect, these military feats—more than twenty-five years before his nomination for President—were the high points of Harrison's career. He served two undistinguished terms in Congress and part of a term in the United States Senate. In 1829, Henry Clay, then Secretary of State, procured his appointment as minister to Colombia, where he offended the government of his host country. He then returned to his farm at North Bend, Ohio. He had made a number of unfortunate investments and eked out a living with the help of his salary as county recorder for Hamilton County, Ohio. He ran as one of several Whig candidates for President in 1836 and immediately began preparing to run again in 1840.

Democrats were quick to ridicule Harrison, saying that he wanted nothing more than to spend the rest of his days in a log cabin with a barrel of hard cider. But these criticisms backfired;

two Whig operatives in Pennsylvania put together a huge transparency of a log cabin with a cider barrel by the door and displayed the picture on the wall at a political rally. The idea caught fire.

> Conscious that they had a winning formula, Whig party managers avoided the issues, published no party platform, and built their campaign instead around the log cabin. . . . The Whig campaign began officially on Washington's birthday with a gigantic rally at Columbus, Ohio, replete with log cabins, barrels of cider and cannon salutes. A series of great displays followed—at Tippecanoe, Nashville, Boston, and Cincinnati.[3]

The Whigs could not afford to deal in issues because there were many discordant voices within the party. This tactic also benefited their candidate, who was not adept at political give-and-take. Indeed, Nicholas Biddle, head of the Bank of the United States and one of the staunchest Whig supporters, had written to one of the Whig managers during Harrison's 1836 run for the presidency:

> Let him say not one single word about his principles, or his creed—let him say nothing—promise nothing. Let no Committee, no convention—no town meeting ever extract from him a single word, about what he thinks now, or what he will do hereafter. Let the use of pen and ink be wholly forbidden as if he were a mad poet in Bedlam.[4]

The Whig campaign—with its mottoes of "Tippecanoe and Tyler Too" and "Van, Van, Is a Used Up Man," and its symbols of log cabin and hard cider caught the imagination of the country.

With Harrison established in the public mind as a rugged frontiersman living in rural simplicity in a log cabin, it was easy to portray Van Buren as an effete Easterner, living in urban elegance in a mansion. While Harrison drank hard cider from an earthenware mug, Van Buren supposedly drank French wine from a silver goblet.[5]

In November, Harrison received 234 electoral votes to Van Buren's 60. Van Buren carried only seven of the twenty-six states that were then in the Union, and lost even his home state of New York by a margin of 13,000.

Tilden's principal contribution to the campaign was an address in October entitled "Prices, Currency, and Wages," which attracted favorable attention from students of the subject. Perhaps in another campaign it might have made a difference, but Tilden's cool, logical approach—which would serve him so well as a lawyer—was politically tone deaf in the emotional campaign of 1840.

Tilden met and talked with Van Buren when the defeated President stopped in New York on his way to Lindenwald, his estate near Kinderhook. He then finally finished his studies and was admitted to the practice of law before the New York courts in 1841. Now he would come into his own. Denied a normal boyhood because of health and temperament, his career as a lawyer would flourish because of his ability to reason persuasively, and his own personal fortune would be made by the shrewdness of his investments.

Tilden began his practice by renting a part of the office of John Edmunds, under whom he had read law before his admission to the bar. He then established his own office at No. 13 Pine Street. He was quickly exposed to a practice familiar to many attorneys: members of his family wished him to handle their claims. The drawback, from the attorney's point of view, of course, is that the family members rarely expect to pay the going rate for services, if indeed they expect to pay anything at all. Tilden's casebook for 1842 showed several court appearances for fees of $10 or $15 each, and the drafting of a will for which he charged $1.

Meanwhile, he continued his active participation in politics, much to the annoyance of his father, who continued to support him financially. The death of his father early in 1842 was a severe blow to the newly minted lawyer. His biographer Flick describes it as

|t|he greatest sorrow of his life. . . . Elam had been the close friend and confidant of his son in all the details of his life. Their letters were long exchanged two and three times a week, and the father's thoughts helped to explain the son's intellectual growth.[6]

In 1843 Tilden—following a pattern similar to that followed by Hayes in Cincinnati—sought the office of corporation counsel of New York City. He received strong backing from the local leaders of the Democratic Party, and was chosen for the office by a vote of 20 of the 26 city councilmen. Suddenly his practice was transformed into a highly responsible position giving legal representation to the largest city in the United States.

He processed claims against the city; he issued complaints for violation of city ordinances such as encumbrances on the sidewalks, operating a cab on Sunday, driving at more than five miles per hour, and dumping coal ashes in the street. When the violators refused to pay the fines, he tried their cases in the courts. The office paid $2,500 per year plus such costs of suits as might be awarded by the court. He estimated that he netted a little more than $2,000 for his efforts. After only a year or so of service in the office, he was removed when his political opponents captured the mayor's office.

Tilden had been looking forward to the presidential election of 1844 as an opportunity to elect his friend and mentor Van Buren to a second term. The Whigs were expected to nominate Clay again; Harrison had died after only a month in office, and his Vice President, John Tyler, who succeeded him, had mightily displeased the Whigs during his four years as chief executive.

But now a new question appeared on the political horizon. Texas, originally a province of Mexico settled by southerners from the United States, had revolted against Mexico and obtained its independence in 1836. Now it wished to be annexed to the United States. In the spring of 1844, both Van Buren and Clay, acting independently of one another, issued statements opposing annexation. Tilden praised Van Buren for his position, though it was clear that it antagonized southern Democrats who favored annexation. He joined other Van Buren managers at the Baltimore convention of the Democratic Party in May 1844. He wrote to his brother that the Van Buren forces had a small majority among the delegates, but that there was "excitement and great uncertainty."

The uncertainty was generated by the prospect that the convention would continue to adhere to its "two-thirds" rule: to be nominated, a candidate must have not merely a simple majority of delegates, but an extraordinary majority of two-thirds. This rule, originally adopted at the 1832 convention to help the Jackson–Van Buren ticket, now threatened to defeat Van Buren's candidacy. The convention did adopt the two-thirds rule, and indeed every Democratic convention until 1936 followed that practice. Van Buren had a majority, but not a two-thirds majority; through eight ballots it became clear that he could not attain that majority, and on the ninth James K. Polk of Tennessee was nominated—the first "dark horse" or outsider candidate in American history.

Even though Polk had beaten out Van Buren for the nomination, Tilden worked hard for the Democratic ticket in New York. Polk favored annexation, but behind this question was a more troubling question of the expansion of slave states in the Union. The southerners who settled Texas had brought the institution of slavery with them, and it was clear that the admission of Texas would result in at least one (and, because of its size, perhaps more than one) new slave state.

That summer Tilden joined with his longtime friend and fellow Democrat John L. O'Sullivan to establish a newspaper which could be the voice of the Democratic Party in New York City. They obtained financial backing from wealthy sympathizers and put out the first issue of their newspaper in August 1844. Tilden's association with the paper guaranteed that it would speak with a certain amount of authority on political issues. The *New York Morning Daily News,* as it was called, vigorously espoused the election of the national and state Democratic tickets and was given credit for helping carry New York for Polk by the slim margin of 5,000 votes. Had Polk not won New York, Clay would have been elected President. After the *Morning News* had accomplished this purpose, Tilden lost interest in it and turned over his shares to O'Sullivan. Two years later, the *Morning News* was defunct for lack of advertising.

Tilden would now take a steadily more important part in the political life of New York and of the nation. The leaders of the Albany Regency dispatched him to Washington to advise Polk of its wishes for the cabinet position which would almost certainly go to New York. It was the most populous state, and it had been crucial to Polk's victory over Clay. But the Democrats in the

Empire State were once again feuding, and the harassed Polk did not accede to their wishes.

Tilden was a successful candidate for the State Assembly—the lower house of the New York legislature—in 1845. The following year he was elected a delegate to the New York State Constitutional Convention. He served there constructively and became acquainted with influential businessmen, many of whom would later become his clients. At the end of his term in the Assembly, he refused offers to stand for the State Senate and for Congress, wishing to return to the full-time practice of his profession. While his practice remained general for a time, he turned more and more to business clients. His fees were modest, even by the standards of his own day. His fee for merging a coal company with a small railroad, for example, was $175. Clients also sought his advice about investments in various enterprises with which he was familiar. By 1850 he was prosperous, if not wealthy.

Though not holding public office during this period, he remained active in Democratic Party affairs. He was a leader of the Barnburner faction of the party, which was opposed by the Hunker faction. The Barnburners resisted the extension of slavery into the territories and supported the Wilmot Proviso, which would have prevented slavery in any of the territory acquired as a result of the Mexican War. The Hunker faction, on the other hand, preferred not to take such a position in deference to the southern wing of the Democratic Party.

In 1848 Tilden was one of the leaders in the affairs of the newly formed Free Soil Party, which nominated his old friend Van Buren as a third-party presidential candidate in that year. The party's theme was opposition to the extension of slavery into territories which had not yet been admitted as states. Van Buren received 10 percent of the popular vote, and his candidacy was a harbinger of the formation of the Republican Party during the next decade. Tilden stayed with the Democrats after the election of 1848. His advice was sought by many, including Franklin Pierce after he was elected President in 1852.

As Tilden became prosperous, his social life greatly expanded. He was by no means a gregarious backslapper but a witty conversationalist much in demand for society dinner parties. He became more at ease with women and at one point compiled a list of women whose company he enjoyed. His name was linked with at least one eligible lady, but he never took the plunge. His biographer describes him in these words:

> At this period Tilden was of medium height, slender rather than thin, with a quick nervous walk and gesture, erect and self-important and with a face that would arrest attention in a crowd. His round, well-formed countenance reflected intelligence, mental alertness and contentment. His brow was high and wide, indicating the student, his light blue eyes were large, wide apart, slow moving, and penetrating. His chin was square and showed stubbornness. His mouth was the least attractive part of his round face and its character was due to the early loss of teeth. . . . He was fond of appearing in a Prince Albert coat because it accentuated his height and weight, and a high stiff collar with a long black bow tie. His shoes were small and nicely polished. All in all his appearance was that of a man of importance, and yet for some reason his clothes never seemed to fit him quite right.[7]

His legal work was now becoming much more of a corporate practice, and his earnings came not merely from fees but from participation in profitable corporate reorganizations. He represented William Ogden, a transplanted New Yorker and Chicago railroad magnate, in a series of railroad mergers and acquisitions which resulted in the formation of the Chicago & Northwestern Railroad in 1859. This line became one of the leading railroads in the upper Midwest; Tilden took his fee in securities, and thereby went from being merely prosperous to wealthy.

He took his second fling at elective office when he ran unsuccessfully for state attorney general in 1855. The political winds in the nation were beginning to shift. For the preceding quarter-century the two major parties had been the Whigs and the Democrats. But in 1854 the Republican Party had arisen in the Midwest as a protest against the enactment of the Kansas–Nebraska Act by Congress. Now another party sprang up—the Native American Party—in protest against what it regarded as a flood of new immigrants from Europe. There were two rival Democratic tickets in the state election of 1855, together with a joint Whig-Republican ticket, a Native American ticket, and several minor parties as well. The Native American Party—referred to as "Know-Nothings" because when a member was asked about the party's beliefs he would answer "I know nothing"—carried the state, sending Tilden back to his law practice in New York City.

The following year, the Republican candidate for President, John C. Frémont, carried New York by 80,000 votes. He lost nationwide to James Buchanan, but the latter won only a minority of the popular vote. That vote was split three ways among Buchanan, Frémont, and the Native American candidate Millard Fillmore. Both Buchanan and his predecessor, Franklin Pierce, were known as "doughfaces"—northern men who sympathized with the southern proslavery wing of the Democratic Party. In 1860 the northern wing would rebel against this orientation, and as a result the party would split in two.

Its convention in 1860 was held in Charleston, South Carolina, but because of the "two-thirds" rule the delegates could not agree upon a candidate. Stephen Douglas, the leading northern Democrat, had antagonized the southern wing by rejecting its more extreme demands. Members of this wing wanted Kansas admitted to the Union with a constitution which had been adopted under a set of rules slanted in favor of slaveholders; Douglas, the champion of "popular sovereignty," balked. He likewise resisted their demand for congressional action which would affirmatively protect slavery in the territories.

The Charleston convention adjourned without having made a nomination, to reconvene later in Baltimore where Douglas was chosen after most of the southern delegates had walked out. These delegates held their own convention and picked John C. Breckenridge, a southerner and Buchanan's Vice President, as their candidate. Meanwhile, in Chicago, the Republicans had rejected William H. Seward, former Governor of New York and now senator from that state, in favor of the lesser-known Abraham Lincoln. A fourth party, the Constitutional Union Party, now formed, seeking to bridge the gap between North and South by saying nothing about the issues of the day, and nominating John Bell of Tennessee.

Tilden had been active behind the scenes that spring, because he was concerned that Lincoln's election would lead to the breaking up of the Union. Lincoln's name was not even on the ballot in most southern states, and he had no chance of carrying any of them. He would, Tilden thought, be a completely sectional President, to whom the South would have no attachment.

The Democratic Party in New York was once again split between the "Hards" (formerly Hunkers) and the "Softs" (formerly Barnburners). Frantic efforts were made to agree on a fusion ticket which both factions could support. Tilden was active in these negotiations and prepared an elaborate address on the issues facing the country. He concluded that the southerners, "determined to preserve the social superiority of their race," would never accept the Republican doctrine on that subject—that their peculiar institution was permissible in the states where it existed but could not be extended into any of the territories such as Kansas and Nebraska. If Lincoln were elected, it would mean secession. But if Lincoln were defeated, Tilden reasoned, the North would be less disappointed by the defeat than the South would be by his election. The South, he thought, was absolutely determined to keep and extend slavery, even at the cost of secession; the northern opposition to slavery, he thought, was less deeply felt.

Tilden was certainly correct about the South, but he was wrong in believing that northerners in general did not feel strongly about the issue of slavery. The abolitionist movement, begun by men such as William Lloyd Garrison in Boston a generation earlier, demanded that slavery be abolished *now*. It had first appealed only to a tiny fraction of the populace of that city. But the Kansas–Nebraska Act, the treatment of "Bleeding Kansas" by Presidents Pierce and Buchanan, and the Dred Scott decision by the Supreme Court in 1857 had profoundly stirred up slavery as an issue in the nation. If the growing, but still small, number of abolitionists were coupled with those who opposed the extension of slavery to the territories, they were a majority in the North—as the election of 1860 would prove. And they did feel deeply about the issue. They believed that during the 1850s the North had been bullied by the South in all three branches of the national government—the executive, the legislative, and the judicial—and they resented it.

New York Democrats finally agreed on a state fusion ticket, which was indeed a strange hybrid. If this ticket received a majority of the votes, 18 of the state's electoral votes would go to

Douglas, 7 to Breckenridge, and 10 to Bell. Tilden worked hard but in vain for this ticket. On November 7, Lincoln carried the state by 35,000 votes. He received a majority of the electoral vote nationally, but only a minority of the popular vote. Of that, he received about 40 percent, with the remainder being spread among Douglas, Breckenridge, and Bell.

After Lincoln's election, Tilden urged a conciliatory policy on the new administration. He said that "he for one would resist, under any circumstances, the use of force to coerce the South into the Union."[8] But after the Confederates fired on Fort Sumter in April 1861, he agreed that the Union cause must be supported.

In the congressional elections of 1862, the Democrats made significant gains throughout the North because of dissatisfaction with the way the Lincoln administration was conducting the war. Tilden was instrumental in recruiting his old ally, Horatio Seymour, as the Democratic candidate for Governor in New York. After a bitter campaign, Seymour was elected by a margin of 10,000 votes. In 1863, the National Draft Act aroused strident opposition in New York City, and Seymour made an intemperate speech to a mass meeting on July 4. He compared Lincoln to King Charles I and denounced military conscription as unconstitutional. Only days afterward, the actual commencement of the draft was marked by riots in New York City which led to the loss of life and destruction of property. Tilden thought the validity of the Draft Act should be tested in the courts, but he played no part in the riots.

After the Civil War ended in Union victory, Tilden supported Andrew Johnson, a War Democrat who had succeeded to the presidency when Lincoln was assassinated in April 1865. Johnson broke with the radical element of the dominant Republican Party over the manner in which the former Confederate states should be treated. When it came time for another presidential election in 1868, Tilden was chairman of the New York State Democratic Party. Johnson was a candidate for the nomination, even though he had been elected on the "Union" ticket with Lincoln in 1864. But he had just barely avoided removal from office as a result of his impeachment trial in 1868, and the Democrats were inclined to look elsewhere.

Chief Justice Salmon P. Chase eagerly sought the Democratic nomination, and Tilden seems to have favored him, though not openly. The Democratic convention was held in New York City, and after elaborate maneuvering and horse trading Horatio Seymour received the nomination on the twenty-first ballot. The party leaders were anything but elated with the ticket of Seymour and Frank Blair of Missouri for Vice President. S.L.M. Barlow, a party leader in New York, said, "Our ticket creates almost universal execration," whereas Kate Chase Sprague, having managed the unsuccessful campaign of her father, Chief Justice Chase, said, "I fear that when the South seceded the brains of the party went with it."[9]

Tilden, as surprised as any by Seymour's nomination, nonetheless managed the campaign. The Democrat lost badly to Grant in the Electoral College, but came within 300,000 of the Republican victor in the popular vote.

If we compare Tilden's career with that of Hayes in 1868, they bear little resemblance to each other. Hayes was in the midst of his first term as Governor of Ohio, after an impressive military career in the Civil War and a lackluster two terms in the House of Representatives. He was married with a growing family. Tilden, by contrast, was very much a mover and shaker in the national Democratic Party. He had made a fortune as a corporate lawyer, but sat out the Civil War and never married.

Tilden now turned his attention to corruption in New York.

There were targets aplenty. The infamous Tweed Ring began to operate in New York City even before the Civil War. William Marcy Tweed was elected to the City Common Council in 1851, which under his tutelage would come to be known as the "Forty Thieves." He became a sachem of Tammany Hall, the political organization which was the mainstay of the Democratic Party in the city. He succeeded in having John T. Hoffman elected Governor, and his henchman Oakley Hall elected mayor.

The Ring decided that all municipal contracts should be let in an amount at least double the sums that would actually be paid for work done, with the balance to be divided among the politicians. By 1870, *Harper's Weekly* and its cartoonist, Thomas Nast, began an exposé of the Ring. They were soon joined by the *New York Times*. They showed, for example, that the new county courthouse would cost $12 million, but that two-thirds of that amount was siphoned off as graft by the Ring and its allies. The amount which the Ring ultimately stole from the city was variously estimated at from $30 million to $200 million.

As a fellow Democrat, Tilden was on friendly terms with the Ring. But he grew disenchanted with its political tactics, not so much on moral grounds as that its activities were contrary to the best interests of the Democratic Party. By the fall of 1871, he was openly demanding that the Ring be exposed and its members be removed from public office. In the municipal election of 1871, reformers overwhelmingly defeated the Ring candidates. Tweed was arrested and charged with forgery and grand larceny. He was tried in January 1873, represented by no less than eight lawyers, including the young Elihu Root and David Dudley Field. Tilden testified against him at the trial, which was long, bitter, and resulted in a hung jury. At a second trial Tweed was convicted, fined, and sentenced to twelve years' imprisonment. Two years later, he escaped and fled first to Cuba and then to

Spain. Tilden, by then Governor of New York, successfully sought his extradition; he was returned to New York City, where he died in prison in 1878.

Tilden had been urged in 1874 by several groups to seek the Democratic nomination for Governor. He was nominated by the state convention in September and defeated his Republican opponent, incumbent John A. Dix, in November. He carried reform credentials with him to Albany, and now his attention turned to the Canal Ring. That organization was to political grafters in upstate New York what the Tweed Ring had been to their counterparts in New York City. The Erie Canal, completed in 1825, had played a significant part in drawing the commerce of the Midwest to the port of New York rather than to other East Coast ports. But the canal required constant repair and occasional enlargement, which activities were placed by law in the hands of a Canal Board. Through the use of rigged bids, officials of both political parties profited from kickbacks paid on exorbitantly high contracts for labor and materials. Tilden appointed a bipartisan commission to investigate the activities of the Ring; the commission's conclusions were a devastating bill of particulars against the canal managers. Several members of the Ring were indicted and its power was finally broken.

The reform efforts of New York's Governor during 1875 and 1876 were cited by the Democrats as a welcome contrast to the scandals of the Grant administration. The New York State Democratic Convention meeting in Utica in 1876 endorsed Tilden as its candidate for President. The Governor and his allies went to work at once, forming a Newspaper Popularity Bureau, well staffed with writers. They sent out paid advertisements to local newspapers nationwide, and also favorable press clippings. The Tilden "boom" was under way.

A cloud on the otherwise sunny horizon of the national

Democratic Party was the monetary issue. Grant, it will be recalled, had signed a law pledging to redeem greenbacks in specie over a period of time. But the hard times which followed the Panic of 1873 had increased the demand for soft money, so that debtors could repay their creditors with inflated dollars. The monetary issue broke not so much along political party lines as along geographic ones: debtors tended to be in the West, creditors in the East. But there were more soft-money Democrats than there were Republicans.

The Democratic National Convention met in St. Louis in late June 1876—two weeks after the Republican National Convention which had nominated Hayes. Tilden's most formidable rival for the first prize was Governor Thomas A. Hendricks of Indiana. As a senator during Reconstruction, he had opposed both the Thirteenth and the Fourteenth Amendments to the Constitution, and also opposed the conviction of President Johnson. But now he stood principally for a soft-money policy. Tilden, on the other hand, true to his eastern connections, believed in hard money. On the first ballot in St. Louis, Tilden received 404½ votes—a majority, but not the necessary two-thirds—to Hendricks' 140½, with the rest scattered to others. Tilden was nominated on the next ballot, and the following day the convention unanimously nominated Hendricks for Vice President.

— CHAPTER 4 —

Since the watershed election of 1860, Republican strength had been concentrated in the North and Democratic strength in the South. The Republican Party had its greatest edge in New England and in the upper Midwest, while the populous band of industrial states stretching from New York to Illinois were usually the political battleground.

These sectional divisions had not been nearly as sharp before the Civil War. In 1856 James Buchanan, the Democratic candidate, had carried New Jersey, Pennsylvania, Illinois, Maryland, Kentucky, and Missouri as well as the soon-to-be Confederate states. In 1852, Franklin Pierce's Democratic victory swept every state but four—Vermont, Massachusetts, Kentucky, and Tennessee. And in 1848, the Whig candidate Zachary Taylor defeated Democrat Lewis Cass while losing every one of the states which made up the old Northwest Territory: Ohio, Indiana, Illinois, Michigan, and Wisconsin.

In 1868, however, Ulysses S. Grant had been elected by the votes of all of the northern states except New York, New Jersey, and Oregon, together with all of the southern states except Kentucky, Georgia, and Louisiana. But these figures were skewed because most of the southern states were undergoing some form of reconstruction, and Virginia and Mississippi had not yet been readmitted to the Union. The results in 1872 followed a similar pattern.

But by 1876, the prospects of a Republican presidential candidate carrying any southern state were considerably dimmer. Republican success there depended on the votes of the newly freed slaves, and the Fifteenth Amendment forbidding denial of the right to vote on the basis of race was not very effective in securing their franchise. In many places the Ku Klux Klan and similar organizations carried on a successful campaign of violence and threats against these voters, either dissuading or preventing them from going to the polls. How determinative these efforts would be in the presidential election might affect the outcome in an otherwise close vote.

Hayes and Tilden would contend for the electoral votes of the thirty-eight states then in the Union. The four states with the most electoral votes were New York (35), Pennsylvania (29), Ohio (22), and Illinois (21). Of these, New York had gone Democratic in 1868, but Republican in 1872. The other three had voted Republican both times. It is interesting to note the contrast between the four electoral prizes in 1876 and in 2000. In the latter year, California led with 54 electoral votes, followed by New York with 33, Texas with 32, and Florida with 25. In 1876, California had 6, Texas had 8, and Florida had 4.

Presidential campaigns in the nineteenth century were quite different from those of today. Not only was there no radio or television, but the candidates themselves did not go on the campaign trail. They generally stayed home and relied on surrogates crisscrossing the country to get out their message. Indeed, it was not until 1896 that Williams Jennings Bryan, the Democratic nominee for President, visited cities across the country to seek votes.

Perhaps because of this reticence on the part of the candidates, considerable attention was paid to the somewhat formalistic ritual of their acceptance letters. The candidate did not accept the nomination at the convention, as today, but several weeks afterward. A group representing the national party called on him to "notify" him of his nomination—of which, of course, he was already aware. The candidate then issued an acceptance letter, declaring to no one's surprise that he was pleased to accept the party nomination.

Hayes' letter was made public on July 8. He stressed his commitment to thoroughgoing reform of the civil service, and his commitment to resumption of specie payments—i.e., the redemption of greenbacks with gold. He also made a somewhat equivocal statement about the future of the South, recognizing the need for southerners to control their own affairs but calling for respect for the constitutional rights of all citizens.

Tilden's letter was not released until July 31. The Democratic convention had come after the Republican, and Tilden labored over his document for nearly three weeks. He, too, promised a complete reform of the federal civil service. He also emphasized the need for frugality in government. Like Hayes, he endorsed the resumption of specie payments. His position on this issue was more difficult than Hayes' because Thomas Hendricks, his vice presidential nominee, was an avowed opponent of specie resumption. Hendricks was an ardent Greenbacker, and his views were endorsed by a large number of voters in the Midwest and West. These views, in turn, caused great consternation among Tilden's supporters in the eastern establishment. New York editor Whitelaw Reid, writing to John Bigelow, Tilden's close associate, on July 9, said: "It does not seem to me by any means clear that he [Tilden] will not be elected. If he is, we ought all to pray night and day that his health may be preserved to protect us against Hendricks."[1]

But Tilden was unequivocal in his call for resumption of specie payments. Hendricks, not to be silenced, issued his own acceptance of the vice presidential nomination, stoutly opposing any resumption.

There was actually a presidential candidate of the Greenback Party on the ballot in nearly twenty states—Peter Cooper of New York. In the forthcoming election he would receive fewer than 100,000 of the nearly 8½ million votes cast. But the Greenback Party's candidate four years later would garner more than twice that number. And in 1892, running on the ticket of the Populist Party (which incorporated the views of the Greenback Party), General James Weaver of Iowa would receive nearly 1 million votes and win the electoral votes of Colorado, Idaho, and Kansas. The party disappeared from the ballot in 1896, when the Democratic Party adopted a large part of its program.

The national headquarters of both parties were located in New York City, which allowed Tilden to personally direct his campaign in a way in which Hayes could not from Ohio. The Democratic National Committee had chosen Abram Hewitt as its chairman. Hewitt was a businessman and a recently elected member of Congress, but something of a novice in politics. He was nominally in charge of the Tilden campaign, but in fact the nominee ran things—a highly organized and effective effort.

The Publicity Bureau of the pre–St. Louis days morphed into the Literary Bureau, which produced reams of favorable material to be sent out to city and rural newspapers throughout the country. Its masterpiece was a 750-page campaign textbook, excerpts from which, describing in lurid and partisan detail the scandals of the Grant administration, were reprinted in thousands of newspapers and periodicals.

There was also a Speakers' Bureau, headed by Tilden's nephew, Colonel W. T. Pelton. This body matched available ora-

Justice David Davis, painted before 1947 from earlier portraits.

tors with requests from local campaign organizations. Tilden clubs were assembled to provide parades and audiences for the speakers. All of this, of course, required money—though not of the magnitude spent in today's campaigns. Tilden's biographer Flick estimated the amount raised by the national committee as approaching $500,000. Tilden could, of course, have easily contributed this amount himself, but he was understandably loath to do so when there were other wealthy Democratic resources available.

Hayes' campaign got off to a bad start because of rivalries within the party in New York State. Senator Roscoe Conkling, the Republican boss of the state, had replaced former Governor Edwin Morgan, an excellent fund-raiser, with a Customs House toady, Alonzo Cornell, as the New York representative on the national committee. The members of the committee loyal to Grant and Blaine had selected Secretary of the Interior Zachariah Chandler as its chairman, rather than Hayes' choice, former Governor Edward F. Noyes of Ohio. Such a situation could not occur today, of course, since the choice of chairman of the national committee is regarded as the indisputable prerogative of the presidential candidate.

Chandler himself was opposed to civil service reform, and his method of raising money for the party depended heavily on the traditional levy on federal employees. He did not devote himself totally to the campaign and rarely communicated with Hayes. While a man of considerable means, Hayes did not possess the liquid assets to make a significant contribution to the party funds, and the bleak prospects of the Republican ticket made it difficult to raise money elsewhere.

Hayes determined that it was essential to once more "wave the bloody shirt"—to impress on the electorate that while every Democrat had not been a rebel, every rebel had been a Democrat. This view was captured in its positive aspect by the speech which Governor Noyes made when placing Hayes' name in nomination before the Cincinnati convention:

"... I have the honor to present the name of a Gentleman well known and favorably known throughout the country.

One held in high respect and much beloved by the people of Ohio. A man who during the dark and stormy days of the rebellion, when those who are invincible in peace and invisible in war were uttering brave words to cheer their neighbors to the fore-front of battle, followed his leaders and his flag until the authority of our Government was reestablished from the lakes to the gulf, and from ocean to ocean. . . ."[2]

Hayes' war record was obviously a political asset with northern voters. But the Republicans also sought to paint a negative picture of Tilden's conduct during the Civil War. He had remained a civilian throughout the war. He was overage for the draft and, indeed, it is difficult to imagine anyone more out of place in the rank and file of the Army than Samuel Tilden, even at a young age. And even younger, politically successful men in the north had remained civilians. James G. Blaine, the odds-on favorite for the Republic nomination at the Cincinnati convention, had paid to hire a substitute (as the law allowed) when he was drafted.

Tilden had supported the northern war effort openly, if not enthusiastically. But the Republicans attempted to tie him to the infamous 1864 "peace plank" in the Democratic national platform. The "peace Democrats" had gained control of that convention, and one of the planks in the platform declared the northern war effort a failure, called for an armistice, and for a convention of all the states to restore the Union. The convention nominated General George McClellan as its candidate for President to oppose Lincoln, but in the November election he won the electoral votes of only three of the twenty-five states that voted.

Tilden had attended the 1864 convention as a member of the New York delegation that had voted for McClellan, and Tilden had contributed money and time to his campaign. But when the peace plank was attributed to him by Republicans in 1876, he was able to show that he had urged McClellan to renounce it.

Tilden was also attacked for having filed fraudulent income tax returns, and for having grown wealthy on the corpses of dead railroads. The facts in each case were complicated and somewhat ambiguous. Certainly no criminal liability was established, but there was some damage to the candidate.

In October, a month before the election, Ohio and Indiana held state elections for Governor and other officials. Returns from these contests buoyed the Democrats. Their Democratic candidate for Governor in Indiana, James Douglas "Blue Jeans" Williams, defeated the Republican Benjamin Harrison by a margin of about 5,000 votes. The last time Indiana had voted for a Democrat in a presidential election was twenty years earlier, in 1856. The Republican candidate for Governor in Ohio won by 10,000 votes. The last time Ohio had gone Democratic in a presidential election was in 1852, before the birth of the Republican Party.

No PRESIDENTIAL ELECTION day dawns bright and clear everywhere in the United States, and November 7, 1876, was no exception. Weather has always been a factor in predicting the outcome of elections, as is reflected by an article in the *New York Herald* on election day that was devoted entirely to the weather nationwide:

> The weather has frequently exercised a powerful influence in determining the results of popular elections. It has grown into a popular belief that fair weather is good for the Republican Party, and that bad weather is favorable to the Demo-

crats. Why this should be it is not difficult to understand, especially in the case of the larger cities of the East. The Republican ranks are largely recruited from the wealthier classes of the community, the men who live in comfortable houses and wear good clothes. On the other hand, the laborers, the men who earn small wages and work with their hands, form the bone and sinew of the Democratic masses. But these conditions do not prevail equally over the Union. In the West, the farming classes, the hearty pioneers of civilization, frequently form the Republican strength, while the professional men and those engaged in trade form that of the Democratic Party. The Southern proprietors and businessmen, like the Western, are by tradition and condition Democratic, while their laborers are in the opposition ranks. In the East and North, we are importers and manufacturers. In the West and South production and exportation form the bases of prosperity. The election today will no doubt be similarly influenced throughout the country by the state of the weather, as have former elections, and with a view to informing the readers of the *Herald* on such an interesting subject we present the following series of "weather probabilities" for the several states, which are arranged in alphabetical order. . . .

The article went on to predict warm and cloudy weather with rain along the entire eastern seaboard, cold and clear weather in the Midwest and in the plains states, and clear temperate weather on the Pacific slope. The paper also carried an interview with President Grant in which he predicted that Tilden would carry most of the South, Hayes most of the North, and that Hayes would win by a margin of some 50 electoral votes.

The *Herald* also published accounts of activities at the headquarters of the two parties in New York City.

AT THE DEMOCRATIC HEADQUARTERS

The confidence shown at the rooms of the Democratic Central Committee, at the Everett House, all day yesterday, was remarkable. The Democratic Committee was apparently as certain of victory as though the result had been once for all decided. Mr. Magone spoke in no uncertain tones.

"I tell you," said he, with impressive earnestness, "that it is too late for any further appeals and arguments. The fiat has gone forth, and as sure as the sun will rise and set tomorrow, Governor Tilden will be elected by a magnificent majority."

AFFAIRS AT REPUBLICAN HEADQUARTERS

The following dispatch was received from Mississippi on the condition of affairs there:

Holly Springs, Miss.
November 6, 1876.
To Hon. Z. Chandler, Chairman:—

I am in possession of facts which warrant me in saying that the election in the northern half of this State will be a farce. Colored and white Republicans will not be allowed to vote in many of the counties. The Tilden clubs are armed with Winchester rifles and shotguns, and declare that they will carry the election at all hazards. In several counties of my district leading white and colored Republicans are

now refugees asking for protection. . . . A reign of
terror such as I have never before witnessed exists in
many large Republican counties to such an extent
that Republicans are unable to cope with it. If it were
not for rifles and shotguns this State would give
Hayes and Wheeler from 20,000 to 30,000 majority. I
send this dispatch from Holly Springs, because it is
impossible to rely on the Oxford office.

J. H. PIERCE,
United States Marshal.
Northern District of Mississippi.

The *Herald* also printed a story datelined Washington dealing with betting on the election in the nation's capital:

POOL SELLING AT WASHINGTON
Washington, Nov. 6, 1876.
Pool selling here to-night amounted to very little, notwithstanding an order from New York to a prominent betting
man to place $2,000 in lots on Tilden at odds of not greater
than 5-to-4. One pool of 100-to-75 on Tilden and half dozen
more at an average of 25-to-20 comprised the night's business, the odds being in favor of Tilden, whose friends were
much encouraged by the rainstorm tonight and a hope of its
continuance tomorrow.

It is said tonight that the Republican plan of campaign
underwent an important change within the past week, and
that while Zach Chandler was apparently working might
and main in New York to carry that State, the forces
and money of the Republican National Committee were

secretly sent to Indiana, the carrying of which state by the party insures the election to Hayes no matter how New York may go.

The *Chicago Tribune* for that day had numerous stories of political activity in different states. The paper was unabashedly Republican and pro-Hayes, as can be seen from its lead column heads:

TO-DAY.

IT WILL DECIDE ONE OF
THE GRAVEST ISSUES OF
THE AGE

WHILE NO MAN CAN TELL
WHAT THE DAY WILL BRING
FORTH,

THERE ARE MANY WISE MEN
WHO PREDICT A REPUBLICAN
VICTORY.

AND THEY FURNISH GOOD
REASONS FOR THE FAITH
THAT IS IN THEM.

REPUBLICAN CONFIDENCE
WAS NEVER MORE
UNWAVERING THAN NOW.

NEW YORK ADVICES VERY
FLATTERING FOR HAYES AND
WHEELER.

———

THE SAME IS TRUE OF
CONNECTICUT, NEW JERSEY,
AND INDIANA.

———

FOUR SOUTHERN STATES SET
DOWN AS SURE TO CHOOSE
HAYES ELECTORS.

———

PROVIDED THE CONFEDERATE
TILDENITES PERMIT A FAIR
AND HONEST ELECTION.

———

THE PROSPECT FAVORABLE
FOR A BIG VOTE IN
CHICAGO.

———

The *Tribune* not only slanted its headlines, but expressly predicted a Hayes victory. The Republican candidate had a good chance of carrying New York, the paper said, if the Democratic majority in New York City could be held below 40,000. Such a victory, along with the success in states more likely to be Republican, would give Hayes 195 electoral votes, 10 more than needed for a majority. In addition, the *Tribune* opined that nine other "doubtful" states were likely to go Republican: South Carolina, North Carolina, Nevada, New Jersey, Indiana, Louisiana, Connecticut, Oregon, and Florida. In fact, New York, New Jersey,

North Carolina, Indiana, and Connecticut would all go Democratic.

The *Tribune* published other stories from across the nation evincing great interest in the election. Kentucky reported that the excitement was intense in every part of the state. So did Tennessee, which expressed justifiable confidence that Tilden would carry the state. Pennsylvania and Massachusetts likewise reported great interest in the election, which each predicted would go to Hayes. The Hayes majority in Pennsylvania was estimated to be between 10,000 and 20,000, while his majority in Massachusetts was expected to be on the order of 30,000. California reported an unprecedented increase in voter registration, with the city of San Francisco alone likely to cast 40,000 votes.

None of these accounts claimed to be in any way based on a public opinion poll. Reports of private wagers, and quite unscientific polls taken spontaneously within a small group, were all that was available to prognosticators. The *New York Herald* carried a story from a source who had polled his fellow passengers on the New York–Philadelphia Express train, and found a majority for Hayes.

These accounts and stories show the great interest in the presidential election of 1876, and the varied predictions of its outcome. People were prepared for a close vote, but scarcely anyone guessed just how close it would be.

— CHAPTER 5 —

ELECTION DAY IN NEW YORK CITY proved to be rainy, as predicted. Tilden voted in the morning and then spent several hours at Democratic headquarters at Everett House. Well-wishers and party officials confidently predicted his election, and he was in good spirits when he was driven home late in the afternoon. A telegraph line had been run to his elegant residence in Gramercy Park, where he continued to receive visitors. After dinner, he returned to headquarters to study the bulletins containing the election returns.

The Hayes family members gathered at their house in Columbus in a much less optimistic frame of mind. Hearing a report that Tilden would carry New York handily and that the vote in Ohio would be very close, they reconciled themselves to defeat.

At the national headquarters of the two parties in New York, returns began coming in as soon as the polls closed in the states along the eastern seaboard. Returns in that era were reported only by telegraph.

The returns dribbled in sporadically, rather than in clumps as they do now with four standard time zones in the continental

United States. Time zones would be established by the railroads in 1883 and enacted into law in 1918. But in 1876, each sizable city was on its own "sun time." When the sun was exactly overhead in that city, it was 12 noon, regardless of what time it might be in a city fifty miles east or fifty miles west. New York City was twelve minutes ahead of Boston and was slightly more than a minute behind Albany. These differences were little noted so long as travel was by stagecoach or wagon, but with the coming of the passenger trains and their fixed schedules, much confusion resulted. Thus the initiative for standard time zones came from the railroads.

All of the New England states except Connecticut—Maine, Vermont, New Hampshire, Massachusetts, and Rhode Island—were carried by Hayes, but by considerably smaller margins than Grant's in 1872. Connecticut, which had gone narrowly for Grant in 1872, now went even more narrowly for Tilden. Though he won only one of these six states, the returns from this Republican stronghold were auspicious for the New Yorker.

Tilden carried his home state by a margin of some 30,000 votes, and neighboring New Jersey by a similar margin. Both of these states had gone for Grant in 1872. Pennsylvania remained narrowly Republican, but Delaware switched. South of the Mason-Dixon Line, the only Republican hopes were in Florida, South Carolina, and Louisiana, where President Grant had sent troops the preceding day.

In the Midwest, it was a different story. Hayes carried both his home state and Illinois by narrow margins, but lost Indiana by an equally close vote. In the upper Midwest, and in Nebraska, Kansas, and Colorado, it was a Republican sweep. Finally the Pacific slope was heard from, and Hayes won both California and Oregon.

The complete returns—with South Carolina, Florida, and

Louisiana uncertain—seemed to presage a Tilden victory. But though the polls had closed throughout the country, the election was not over. General Daniel E. Sickles, on his way home from an after-theater supper, visited Republican headquarters and thought he saw hope amid the gloom. If Hayes could carry South Carolina, Florida, and Louisiana, he could win by one electoral vote.

Sickles' checkered career made him a fitting player to make the first move in the dispute over the election of 1876. He was one of the most remarkable figures in American public life in the nineteenth century. Born in 1819 and living until 1914, he combined considerable ability with considerably more ambition and a hair-trigger temper which led his biographer, W. A. Swanberg, to entitle his volume *Sickles the Incredible*.

Trained as a lawyer, he rose through the ranks of the Tammany machine in New York City to be elected to Congress in 1856 as a Democrat. He took with him to Washington his beautiful child bride, Teresa, whom he had married when she was sixteen. Though a womanizer himself, he was outraged to discover that the United States attorney for the District of Columbia, Phillip Barton Key, a southern patrician in his fifties and a son of Francis Scott Key, was having an affair with Teresa. After waiting for Key to cross Lafayette Square in Washington on the way to his club, Sickles accosted him and then shot him dead.

He was tried for murder and defended by no fewer than eight attorneys, including Edwin M. Stanton, who would later be Lincoln's Secretary of War. His lawyers advanced for the first time in an American trial the claim of "temporary insanity." The jurors agreed, and Sickles was not only acquitted, but cheered by the courtroom crowd, which called for a speech.

Such an escapade would have daunted a lesser ego, but not

Sickles. As soon as the Civil War broke out, he raised a brigade in New York and was commissioned a brigadier general. He saw action in the latter parts of McClellan's peninsular campaign and at Chancellorsville, where he commanded an entire corps. His troops fought valiantly at Gettysburg, but a musket ball in his right leg required its amputation.

Out of the Army, Sickles switched parties and voted for Lincoln's reelection in 1864. Grant appointed him ambassador to Spain, where his headstrong conduct disappointed Secretary of State Hamilton Fish. Resigning from that post, he and his French-speaking second wife settled in Paris. He was only visiting the United States for a few months at the time he became active in the Hayes campaign.

Even though he had no official position in the Republican Party on election night, he audaciously sent out telegrams to its officials in South Carolina, Florida, Louisiana, and Oregon over the name of Zachariah Chandler, the chairman of the national committee:

WITH YOUR STATE SURE FOR HAYES, HE IS ELECTED. HOLD YOUR STATE.

Early editions of morning newspapers proclaimed Tilden the victor. Democratic sheets were exultant as evidenced by the comment of the dyed-in-the-wool *New York World:*

The new era begins. Peace on Earth and to men of good will is the glorious message of this glorious day.[1]

Equally partisan, though Republican, the *Indianapolis Journal* editorialized:

. . . Tilden is elected. The announcement will carry pain to every loyal heart in the nation, but the inevitable truth may as well be stated.[2]

But the *New York Times* refused to concede the election to the Democrats. *Times* news editor John C. Reid had been captured by the Confederates while in the Union Army and confined in the notorious Libby prison, and would not soon forget it. Together with the other members of the editorial board, he pondered what to do. Well after midnight, they received a dispatch from Dan Magone, the chairman of the New York State Democratic Committee, saying: "Please give your estimate of the electoral votes secured for Tilden. Answer at once." The *Times* board realized that this meant that the Democrats were actually in doubt as to Tilden's victory. Edward Cary, a member of the board, wrote an editorial saying that the outcome was doubtful, that Tilden appeared to have 184 electoral votes, Hayes 181, and Florida in doubt.

Before sunrise Reid went to Republican headquarters at the Fifth Avenue Hotel and found it deserted. He was looking for Zachariah Chandler, the national chairman, when he ran into W. E. Chandler, the national committeeman from New Hampshire, dressed in goggles and military greatcoat. Together they canvassed returns from across the nation and figured out how Hayes might win after all. They located the room of Zach Chandler and aroused him from what is varyingly reported to have been a sound sleep or a drunken stupor. They asked his permission to telegraph to leading Republicans in doubtful states— South Carolina, Florida, Louisiana, California, and Oregon. Zach Chandler agreed, and telegrams were accordingly sent, saying that Hayes was elected if they could hold their state—that is, assure that the electoral votes of that state would be cast for Hayes.

By the next morning, many newspapers spoke of a doubtful election, with conflicting claims to the electoral votes of Florida, Louisiana, and South Carolina. It was clear that more voters across the country had voted for Tilden than had voted for Hayes. But this popular vote does not determine the winner of the presidency. It is rather the electoral vote, cast by the presidential electors in each state whose party received a majority of the popular vote in that state. Each state has an electoral vote equal to the number of senators and representatives it is allotted in Congress, and chooses that number of electors to cast its electoral vote in December. But when there is a dispute as to which candidate has won the popular vote of a state, there is a possibility that two competing sets of electors, one from each party, will each cast votes for their respective presidential candidates. The question then becomes who shall decide which set of electoral votes is to be counted.

Article II, Section 1 of the Constitution provides that

> [t]he Electors shall meet in their respective states, and vote by Ballot for two persons. . . . [T]hey shall make a list of all the persons voted for, and the Number of Votes for each, which List they shall sign and certify, and transmit sealed to the Seat of the Government . . . directed to the President of the Senate. The President of the Senate shall, in the Presence of the Senate and House of Representatives, open all the certificates, and the Votes shall then be counted.

The Constitution was silent as to *who* would do the counting. Was it the president of the Senate, or the two houses in joint session? The one constitutional duty assigned to the Vice President was that of presiding over the Senate, but Henry Wilson, Grant's Vice President, had died in 1875. The presiding officer of the Senate now was its president pro-tem, Thomas W. Ferry, a Michigan Republican. The Senate was controlled by the Republicans, and the House by the Democrats.

Hayes and some of his Republican supporters contended that the decision of the Senate president as to which set of returns to count should be final. But this was not the only way to read the constitutional provisions, and the Democrats understandably would have none of it. If there were to be competing election returns, the situation cried out for a political solution.

In 1865, both houses of Congress had adopted Joint Rule 22 governing the counting of the electoral vote. It provided that "no vote objected to shall be counted except by the concurrent vote of the two Houses." This meant that once an objection to an electoral vote was raised, it took a majority in both the House and the Senate to override the objection and count the vote. This rule was in effect when electoral votes were counted in 1865, 1869, and 1873. But in each of those years, the Republicans controlled both houses of Congress, and there was no serious dispute about the outcome of the election.

Early in 1876, in the first session of that Congress—the Senate rescinded Joint Rule 22, and on December 8 of that year, after the dispute as to the election arose, Senator Ferry ruled that it had been repealed, and he was sustained by a vote of 50 to 4. So there was no mechanism available to guide the proceedings of the joint session other than the provisions of the Constitution itself, which provided little guidance.

And looming beyond this question was the provision of Article II, providing that "if no Person have a Majority, then from the five highest on the List the said House shall in like Manner chuse the President. But in chusing the President, the Vote shall be taken by states, the representation from each State having one vote. . . ." The Democrats in the House controlled a sufficient number of state delegations in that body to elect Tilden President should it come to that.

On November 10, President Grant issued an order widely circulated throughout the country. It was addressed to General W. T. Sherman:

> Instruct General Augur, in Louisiana, and General Ruger, in Florida, to be vigilant with the force at their command to preserve peace and good order, and to see that proper and legal Boards of Canvassers are unmolested in the performance of their duties. Should there be any grounds of suspicion of fraudulent counting on either side, it should be reported and denounced at once. No man worthy of the office of President would be willing to hold the office if counted in, placed there by fraud; either Party can afford to be disappointed in the result, but the country cannot afford to have the result tainted by the suspicion of illegal or false returns.
>
>   U. S. Grant

Republican "visiting statesmen" journeyed to the contested states, as did their Democratic counterparts, to give what aid they could to the candidates of their respective parties. On November 12, W. E. Chandler arrived in Tallahassee, the capital of Florida. Ex-Governor Noyes of Ohio, John A. Kasson of Iowa, General Lew Wallace (who would later gain literary fame by writing *Ben-Hur* while Governor of New Mexico Territory), and Francis C. Barlow of New York soon followed him there. The Democratic visitors included ex-Governor Brown of Georgia, C. W. Woolley and John F. Coyle of Pennsylvania, and Manton Marble, editor of the *New York World.* Each side interviewed witnesses and collected affidavits to make their case before the State Canvassing Board, a body charged with tallying the returns from the various counties. Nor were their activities confined to mere advocacy; offers of bribes and political patronage were made on both sides.

Louisiana also had its share of "visiting statesmen" from both parties. John Sherman, James A. Garfield, Eugene Hale, and other Republicans headed for New Orleans at the request of Grant himself. Abram Hewitt, Tilden's campaign manager, urged Democratic bigwigs to go there and represent the party's interest. Lyman Trumbull, a former Republican, Samuel J. Randall, Speaker of the House of Representatives, and "Marse Henry" Watterson, editor of the *Louisville Courier-Journal,* heeded his call. Since the state's returning board consisted entirely of Republicans, the Republican delegation expressed its confidence in the fairness and honesty of the board, a confidence which the Democrats made clear they did not share.

Hayes was not in charge of the Republican effort to make him President. He was kept advised of some, but not all, of the activities of his partisans. John Sherman told him of the Democrats' efforts in Louisiana to keep blacks (who would have voted Republican at that time) from voting and assured him that he would be declared the victor there in accordance with the law. Hayes responded uneasily that "we are not to allow our friends to defeat one outrage and fraud by another. There must be nothing crooked on our part."[3] Charles Farwell, a wealthy Chicago merchant and political insider, very likely paid money to one or more of the members of the Louisiana Returning Board so that it would favor the Republicans.

But Tilden's supporters proved that two could play at that game. An investigation by a congressional committee two years after the election revealed that telegrams in cipher were exchanged between Manton Marble and C. W. Woolley, Tilden agents in Tallahassee, and Colonel W. T. Pelton in New York. Pelton, Tilden's nephew, lived under the same roof with him; he was also secretary of the Democratic National Committee. One of the exchanges read thus:

COL. PELTON, NO. 15 GRAMERCY PARK, N.Y.: CERTIFICATE REQUIRED TO MOSES DECISION HAVE LONDON HOUR FOR BOLIVIA OF JUST AND EDINBURGH AT MOSELLE HAD ANY OVER GLASGOW, FRANCE REC. RUSSIA OF.

The dispatch when translated read:

Have just received a Bolivia |proposition| to hand over at any hour required Russia |Tilden| decision of London |Canvassing Board| and certificate of France |Governor Stearns| for Moselle |two| Glasgow |hundred| Edinburg |thousand|. Moses |Manton Marble|.

To this the following reply came:

TELEGRAM HERE. PROPOSITION TOO HIGH.[4]

December 6 was the day fixed by law for the electors to gather in their respective states and cast their votes. In thirty-four states this ordinarily ministerial function occurred without controversy. But in Florida, South Carolina, Louisiana, and—at the last minute—Oregon—the question was "Which electors?"

The State Canvassing Board in Florida met and began its work in late November.

Of the states which were in dispute, Florida was most different in 1876 from what it is today. Its population in 1870 was 187,248, concentrated in the northern part of the state and mostly rural. (Miami would not even become an incorporated city until 1896.) The population of Key West was 10,000; Jacksonville a little under 7,000; Tallahassee just over 2,000; and Tampa less than 1,000. By 1880, there were about 1,300 miles of railroad track in the state, but concentrated in the northern half. Railroad lines connected points in north Florida with Georgia and Alabama, and a track ran across the neck of the peninsula to connect with ports on both the Atlantic Ocean and the Gulf of Mexico. The railroad would not reach Miami for another twenty years. There were slightly fewer than 50,000 votes cast in the 1876 presidential election, in contrast with the more than 6 million counted in 2000.

The State Canvassing Board at this time consisted of the state attorney general, William Cocke, a Democrat, and Samuel B. McLin and Clayton A. Cowgill, both Republicans. The board's authority went beyond merely counting the returns that were submitted from the various counties of the state. In the 1874 election, Cocke had given an opinion that the board had discretion to exclude returns that were "irregular, false, or fraudulent."

The board began its work in public, and numerous "visiting statesmen" from both parties were allowed to be present. On the face of the returns from the various counties, Tilden led Hayes, but by a margin of only 80-some votes. The board exercised its discretion to reject some of these returns, some unanimously, others by a party-line vote of 2 to 1. It finally concluded that Hayes had won the state over Tilden by a majority of 45 votes.

> What the result would have been if the returns had been canvassed by an unpartisaned board it is impossible to say with certainty. At the same time it is clear that if none of the returns had been rejected and if in Baker County the return containing all the precincts had been substituted for the Driggers return, the result would have been a majority for the lowest Tilden elector over the highest Hayes elector of 93 votes. How nearly these returns corresponded to the votes in the ballot boxes can never be ascertained.[5]

> While a *fair count* of the votes cast in the state of Florida might have resulted in a small majority for Tilden, a *free election* would with far greater certainty have resulted in a substantial majority for Hayes. The Board did not throw out votes, not even single "marked ballots," on the score of intimidation; yet no one familiar with the evidence and with the attitude of the Southern Democrats toward negro suffrage will for a moment doubt that there was sufficient intimidation to change the whole result.[6]

On the basis of the board's conclusion, the Republican electors on December 6 met and cast their votes for Hayes. Results certified by the Governor were sent to the President of the Senate on Washington.

The Democratic electors in Florida, although having no official status, met at the same time as the Republican electors and cast their votes for Tilden. Attorney General Cocke—a Democrat—irregularly certified their result and sent it to the President of the Senate. To complicate matters further, George

C. Drew, the Democratic candidate for Governor, requested the state supreme court to direct the canvassing board to re-count the votes for Governor without exercising any discretion to reject returns. The Democratic-leaning court granted his request, and following the recanvass he was declared Governor.

But the legal proceedings did not stop here. The Democratic presidential electors obtained a ruling from a state trial court that they were the ones properly chosen; this decision was appealed by the Republicans, and the case, of course, became moot after March 4, inauguration day. Finally, in the first week of January 1877, the newly elected Democratic legislature enacted as a first order of business a law creating a new canvassing board to reexamine the November 7 votes. The new board, consisting entirely of Democrats, to no one's surprise declared that Tilden had defeated Hayes by about 90 votes. The legislature then directed that the votes of Democratic electors be certified by the Governor and sent to the President of the U.S. Senate.

In Louisiana the returns from throughout the state on their face gave Tilden a lead of between 8,000 and 9,000. The state had a turbulent history even before the Civil War, and the turbulence increased during the period of Reconstruction. In July 1866, for example, the Radical Republicans attempted to reconvene an earlier constitutional convention in order to enfranchise the freedmen. The mayor of New Orleans sought to suppress the convention; a riot ensued in which about 40 blacks and 1 white Radical were killed and many more wounded. This uprising drew national attention, and was one of the factors which enabled the Radical faction of the Republican Party to gain control of Congress in the election of 1866. The entire period in Louisiana is described by Paul Haworth in these words:

In general the period |from 1868 to 1876| was one in which the party in opposition, consisting of most of the white inhabitants, pursued a policy of intimidation, even to the extent of assassination; while the party in power, consisting chiefly of negros and white carpetbaggers, resorted to election frauds and to unblushing misappropriation of public funds.[7]

The State Returning Board convened on November 17. The board had the same sort of discretion as its Florida counterpart to reject returns for fraud, and even, under some circumstances, where force or intimidation had occurred. The composition of the board was not one to inspire confidence in the Democrats. Its membership was set by law at five, with representation from both parties required. But the one Democrat on the board had previously resigned, and the remaining Republicans had made no effort to replace him. Madison Wells, the president of the board during the Reconstruction regime, had been removed as Governor by General Philip Sheridan for dishonesty. In a letter to Secretary Stanton, Sheridan wrote: "I say now unequivocally that Governor Wells is a political trickster and a dishonest man. . . . His conduct has been as sinuous as the mark left in the dust by the movement of a snake."[8] His fellow members— Thomas Anderson, Louis M. Kenner, and Gadane Casanave— were not held in high regard by impartial observers.

After a closed meeting, the board decided to invite five each of the Republican and Democratic delegations to attend their public meetings. The board received protests, and accepted affidavits in oral testimony. It held twelve public sessions and then retired to reach its decision. During this period rumors circulated that Wells, at least, was for sale to the highest bidder. It was never proved that he took any money. But it may not have been coincidental that Hayes, after he was elected, appointed Wells and two other members of the board to local federal offices. The board released its conclusion two days before the December 6 deadline; it rejected more than 13,000 Democratic and about 2,500 Republican ballots. The result gave Hayes a majority of a little more than 3,000, which was certified and sent to Washington.

On the same day that the returning board announced its decision, Democratic electors met and, on the basis of their own canvass of returns, declared themselves to be the chosen electors and voted for Tilden. Their certificate was signed by John McEnery, who claimed to have been elected Governor in 1874. After pitched street battles and the intervention of federal troops, he had been deposed and replaced by the Republican candidate, William P. Kellogg.

In South Carolina, federal troops had been stationed in various parts of the state ever since the end of the Civil War. Blacks outnumbered whites in the state by a ratio of five to three, and they voted a virtually straight Republican ticket. Often they made up a majority in the legislature. In the summer of 1876, racial hostility lead to the Hamburg Massacre, in which one white man and as many as a dozen blacks were killed, some after they had been captured by an armed posse of whites. Governor Daniel Chamberlain appealed to Grant to send troops into the state in October, and the President obliged.

On election day, there was illegal voting by both white Democrats and black Republicans. The Democrats carried their state ticket, electing Wade Hampton as Governor, but the same ballots gave Hayes a win over Tilden. The Board of Canvassers so certified the returns, outwitting the efforts of the state supreme court to thwart it.

The court thereupon held the members of the board in contempt, fined them $1,500 each, and committed them to the county jail in Columbia, the state capital. They were almost immediately released on writs of habeas corpus by a judge of the federal court.

The historian James Ford Rhodes, writing in 1906, described the situation in the country in the late fall of 1876 in these words:

> The dispute in Congress, in the press and among the people was fierce. The Democrats kept up a persistent cry of fraud but the Republicans retorted that the fraud was on the other side. . . .
>
> No prospect was apparent of their reaching any common ground. . . . Some Senators and Representatives derided the idea of danger; but anyone, who lived through those days in an observing and reflective mood, or anyone, who will now make a careful study of the contemporary evidence, cannot avoid the conviction that the country was on the verge of civil war. The number of men out of employment and in want owing to the depression of business, the many social outcasts in the community, whom the railroad riots seven months later disclosed, constituted a formidable army who were ready for any disturbance that might improve their condition or give them an opportunity for plunder. The mass of adherents on each side, which was clearly indicated by the closeness of the vote in many Northern States, shows what a terrible internecine conflict would have followed a bloody affray on the floor of Congress.[9]

In Oregon, there was no disputing that the Republican electors had been chosen by a margin of about 1,000 votes. But one of the electors, John W. Watts, was a deputy postmaster in a small village a few miles southwest of Portland. He was a fourth-class postmaster and received an annual salary of $268. But Article II, Section 1, of the Constitution provided that no "Person holding an Office of Trust or Profit under the United States shall be appointed an elector." All agreed that Watts was subject to this prohibition. But the state law provided that "if there shall be any vacancy in the office of an elector, occasioned by death, refusal to act, neglect to attend, or otherwise, the electors present shall immediately proceed to fill, by *viva voce* and plurality of votes, such vacancy in the electoral college." The clear intent of this law was that the remaining electors should fill the vacancy.

The Oregon Democrats were slower than their counterparts in the East to exploit this possible opportunity. But they were goaded into action by Tilden agents in New York. The view there was that if one elector in Oregon was a Democrat, the result would force the Republicans to "go behind the returns" sent to Washington and thereby reveal the inconsistency of their position with that taken in Louisiana and Florida. This Oregonian view was embodied in the following telegram sent from Abram Hewitt to Governor L. F. Grover, a compliant Democrat:

UPON CAREFUL INVESTIGATION, THE LEGAL OPINION IS THAT VOTES CAST FOR A FEDERAL OFFICE-HOLDER ARE VOID, AND THAT THE PERSON RECEIVING THE NEXT HIGHEST KNOWN NUMBER OF VOTES SHOULD RECEIVE THE CERTIFICATE OF APPOINTMENT. THE CANVASSING-OFFICER SHOULD ACT UPON THIS, THE GOVERNOR'S CERTIFICATE OF APPOINTMENT BE GIVEN TO THE ELECTOR ACCORDINGLY, AND THE

SUBSEQUENT CERTIFICATE OF THE VOTES
OF THE ELECTORS BE DULY MADE SPECIFY-
ING HOW THEY VOTED. THIS WILL FORCE
CONGRESS TO GO BEHIND THE CERTIFI-
CATE, AND OPEN THE WAY TO GET INTO
MERITS OF ALL CASES, WHICH IS NOT ONLY
JUST, BUT WHICH WILL RELIEVE THE
EMBARRASSMENT OF THE SITUATION.

Not content with giving long-distance advice to Oregon
Democrats, headquarters sent out to that state from Omaha
J.V.H. Patrick. Shortly after he arrived, Patrick sent a cipher
telegram to New York saying it would be necessary to buy the
vote of one of the Republican electors for a price of $10,000.
Money was deposited into Patrick's account, but this particular
scheme was never consummated.

On December 4, the Oregon secretary of state found that the
Republican electors had received the highest number of votes.
But then Governor Grover, who was by law present at the canvass, announced he would hear argument on a Democratic
protest of the result the following day. After argument, he said
that the votes cast for Watts were void and that E. A. Cronin, a
Democrat, should be the third elector. Once more, two sets of
returns—one giving Hayes all three of Oregon's electoral votes,
and the other giving Hayes two and Tilden one—were sent to
Washington. Since Hayes needed every single contested vote to
give him a majority in the electoral college, the loss of Oregon's
one contested vote would be fatal.

The Oregon dispute had the effect that the Democrats hoped
it would as a matter of logic, but as a matter of public relations it
was a serious mistake. If the Republicans insisted that Congress,
or the commission which it appointed, could not consider any

material that had not been contained in the certificate sent to the President of the Senate in states such as Florida and Louisiana, how could they challenge the returns certified by the Governor of Oregon which gave Tilden one of its electoral votes? But if this was a legal coup, it was certainly not a political or public relations victory. With respect to Florida and Louisiana, the Democrats could forcefully argue that a large part of the public thought that Tilden had carried both of the states, and that surely he should not lose them both on what fairly might be thought to be the actions of politically biased Republican returning boards. But the Democratic position in Oregon—clearly contrary to state law—was even more egregious than the Republican position in Florida and Louisiana. Tilden, like Hayes, was playing a no-holds-barred game.

— CHAPTER 6 —

ON MONDAY, DECEMBER 4, two days before the presidential electors in the various states cast their votes, Congress reassembled. The Republican-controlled Senate was presided over by Thomas Ferry of Michigan; Speaker Samuel Randall of Pennsylvania oversaw the Democratic-controlled House. Each House appointed committees to investigate the vote counts in contested states. The House named a special committee and directed its members to go to Florida, Louisiana, and South Carolina to conduct its inquiries. One day later, the Senate Committee on Privileges and Elections was charged with a similar mission, which included not only the states just mentioned, but also Georgia, Alabama, and Mississippi.

The respective committees set out on their journeys to the South where they took voluminous testimony from a great number of witnesses. Each committee issued both a majority and a minority report. The majority of the Senate committee—all Republicans—reported that the electoral votes of Louisiana, Florida, and South Carolina belonged to Hayes. The minority—all Democrats—concluded that they belonged to Tilden. In the House, the majority and minority reports were the exact opposite of those in the Senate. The two houses were at loggerheads; there was no evident way that Congress, following its regular procedures, could resolve the election.

Prominent Democrats assembled in a kind of caucus to plan strategy. Fernando Wood, now a congressman but still remembered as the mayor of New York City who at the beginning of the Civil War had proposed that the city secede from the Union, urged the impeachment of President Grant for illegal use of troops during the election campaign. Some northerners agreed, but several southern members opposed any move that might lead to another civil war. No incendiary measures were approved by the caucus. Meanwhile, Congress received numerous petitions urging it to find a way to resolve the conflict.

Senator George F. Edmunds of Vermont introduced a proposed constitutional amendment authorizing the Supreme Court to decide the contest. The proposal was debated several times in the Senate, but it was never passed. Representative George McCrary of Iowa offered a resolution calling for the appointment of a House committee to work with a similar Senate committee to devise a proposal "to the end that the votes may be counted and the result declared by a tribunal whose authority none can question and whose decision all will accept as final."

The resolution was referred to the House Judiciary Committee, where its fate was uncertain. Tilden opposed any compromise, but he played his cards so close to the vest that his lieutenants were often uncertain of his wishes and therefore unable to work for their attainment. He was not well liked by some of the Democratic power brokers in the House, and this made the task of his lieutenants more difficult.

The Judiciary Committee amended the resolution to call for committees consisting of seven members of each House; this measure passed the House and the following day a similar one passed the Senate. The Senate committee consisted of four Republicans and three Democrats, and the House committee was the partisan mirror image of the Senate committee.

After the Christmas holidays, the two committees began meeting behind closed doors to devise a plan for the peaceful settlement of the dispute. At first members of each party proposed plans obviously favorable to their candidate, plans which were promptly rejected by their opponents. By the middle of January, however, both sides were considering the idea of a commission composed of members of the House, the Senate, and the Supreme Court.

On January 13, a version of the plan was leaked to the public. It called for a commission composed of five House members, five Senate members, and five members from the Supreme Court. It was the choice of the justices which proved the greatest stumbling block. It was simply assumed that the congressional Republicans on the commission would vote for Hayes, and the congressional Democrats would vote for Tilden. It was therefore obvious that the final decision would be made by the votes of the members of the Court.

The original proposal called for five justices to be selected by placing in a hat the names of the six senior justices; one name would be drawn, and the remaining five would serve as members of the commission. Tilden was opposed to any sort of commission, but this proposal particularly incensed him. Not ordinarily a man to coin bons mots, he rose to this occasion, saying "I may lose the Presidency, but I will not raffle for it."[1]

Tilden disliked the whole idea of the commission, because it represented a compromise which he thought unwise. He wished to adhere to a simple strategy that he felt would ensure him victory. Make no concessions now; let the votes be counted as they might be in accordance with the Constitution, even though Senator Ferry might claim the authority to count them himself, and resolve doubtful issues in favor of Hayes. The Democrats could maintain that the count was illegal, and that since no candidate had received a majority of the votes cast, the election should be thrown into the House of Representatives. Democrats controlled the House, and they would surely elect him.

This strategy had the merit of simplicity, but it ignored the increasing sentiment in the country for some sort of resolution. Democrats in Congress were well aware of the fact that Grant was not only President, but had been a remarkably successful commanding general. He had said he intended to see his successor inaugurated on March 4—whoever that might be—and if Ferry proceeded to do the counting himself, the President might use troops to ensure that Hayes was inaugurated on that day. A later vote by the House naming Tilden President might well be a recipe for national chaos. The country simply did not want a situation where each candidate grimly refused to budge from his announced position.

Hayes also opposed the commission proposal. He was adamant that the Constitution gave to the President of the Senate—Ferry—the authority to decide which set of returns to count. But seeing that the bill was apt to pass, he did not make his opposition public. Despite the strong desire of most members of each party in Congress to see their candidate elected, most had also come around to the need for some sort of resolution. Congress, thus, took the matter out of the candidates' hands.

Tilden's repudiation of the six-justice lottery bill had killed that version, and several other proposals were vetoed by either Democrats or Republicans. The House committee then recommended that the five senior justices of the Supreme Court—Nathan Clifford and Stephen Field, thought to be sympathetic to the Democrats, Samuel Miller and Noah Swayne, thought to be

Justice Joseph Bradley, painted in 1904 from earlier portraits.

sympathetic to the Republicans, and David Davis, who was regarded as an Independent—should be named to the commission. Milton Harlow Northrup, secretary of the Special Committee of the House of Representatives on this occasion, later wrote:

This precipitated a discussion of the political bias of Justice David Davis. The distinguished Illinois jurist whom Abraham Lincoln had placed on the Supreme bench was thenceforth, till the committees had come to a final agreement, the storm-center of earnest disputation. The Republicans tenaciously argued that Justice Davis was, to all intents and purposes, a Democrat, and that his selection should be charged up against the Democrats. Just as strenuously the Democratic committeemen insisted that he occupied a midway position between the parties, and therefore could with entire propriety serve as the fifth wheel of the commission coach. Senator Edmunds promptly took issue with Mr. Payne's characterization of Justice Davis as an independent. "Judge Davis," said the cynical Edmunds, "is one of those Independents who stand always ready to accept Democratic nominations. It is my observation that such men are generally the most extreme in their partisanship. I would rather intrust a decision to an out-and-out Democrat than to a so-called Independent."

Mr. Springer: Judge Davis is just about as much a Democrat as Horace Greeley was in 1871; he is not and never was a Democrat. His most intimate friends, among whom I may count myself, don't know to-day whether he favored Tilden or Hayes. He didn't vote at all. Our people in Illinois, when he was mentioned for the Presidency, were utterly hostile to his nomination because he was not a Democrat, and had no standing in that party. They only know that he is absolutely honest and fair.[2]

Finally a consensus emerged that two justices favored by the Republicans, and two favored by the Democrats, should be named to the commission, with those four to choose a fifth member. There was an unspoken understanding that this fifth justice would be Davis. The final version named to the commission Clifford of Maine and Field of California, both Democrats, and Miller of Iowa and William Strong of Pennsylvania, both Republicans.

IT WAS QUITE NATURAL for Congress to turn to the justices of the Supreme Court as members of the Electoral Commission. Unless it was to go totally outside of the government, it had little choice. There was no way that Congress itself could resolve the dispute; witness the majority and minority reports from the investigatory committees of the two houses described above. No Democrat in Congress would think for a moment of calling on President Grant as a tiebreaker. The third branch—the judiciary—was chosen by default. This was a dispute; disputes are traditionally resolved by courts. Congress would undoubtedly get credit for creating a body that was capable of resolving the electoral dispute without resort to arms, but what would be the consequences for the individual justices who would serve on the Commission, and for the Court as an institution? A look at the Court's role in its first century will shed light on the part its justices would play in the election dispute.

Article III of the U.S. Constitution provides that the judicial power of the United States "shall be vested in one Supreme Court, and in such inferior courts as the Congress may from time to time ordain and establish." The first Congress established a Supreme Court with a Chief Justice and five associate justices. Later the total membership would expand to nine, briefly to ten, and back to nine by 1876.

For the first decade of its existence, the Court was but a minor player in the system of federal government. During this period, it decided a total of about sixty cases. When the seat of the federal government moved from Philadelphia to Washington in 1801, space for the Supreme Court was completely forgotten until the last minute, when a room in the basement of the new Capitol building was found for it. In that same year John Marshall became Chief Justice and served in that capacity for thirty-four years. During his tenure, he raised the status of the Court from a very junior partner to a genuinely coequal branch of the tripartite federal government.

He was succeeded by Roger B. Taney, appointed by President Andrew Jackson. Taney would preside over the Court for twenty-eight years. From 1801 to 1864, during a period in which there were fifteen Presidents, there were only two Chief Justices. The Taney Court retained the basic outline of the Marshall Court's jurisprudence, but revised it to give more latitude to the states to solve their own problems. By the time of the presidential election of 1856, the Court was a generally respected third branch of government, although much less in the public eye than either the executive or legislative branch. But in the spring of 1857, all of that changed.

On March 6, 1857, the Court handed down its opinion in the ill-starred Dred Scott case. The northern section of the country was growing in population more rapidly than the southern section, so that the northern states were gaining a numerical edge in the House of Representatives. But the Supreme Court, as constituted at that time, was the reverse. Chief Justice Taney was from Maryland; among the associate justices, James Wayne was from Georgia, Peter V. Daniel from Virginia, John Catron from Tennessee, Robert Grier from Pennsylvania, Samuel Nelson from New York, John Campbell from Alabama, Nathan Clifford from Maine, and Benjamin Curtis from Massachusetts. Thus five members of the Court came from states where slavery existed. Any decision, therefore, in a case involving slavery, would be suspect in the eyes of many northerners.

The Dred Scott case originated as a friendly lawsuit in the federal court in St. Louis, in which Scott, a slave, sued his master, a surgeon in the United States Army. He claimed that because his master had taken him away from Missouri and into Illinois, a free state, and then into Wisconsin Territory, a free territory, he had become emancipated even though later returned to Missouri. The lower court ruled against Scott, saying that the law of Missouri governed the effect of his journeys into free states and territories and the Missouri state law said that these journeys did not emancipate him.

This was not a controversial ruling, since it affected only slaves in Missouri. But when Scott appealed the ruling to the Supreme Court, the issues became much broader. On behalf of the master, it was now argued that even though the Missouri Compromise enacted by Congress in 1820 prohibited slavery in all federal territories north of the southern boundary of Missouri, the law was unconstitutional because it prohibited slave owners from bringing their "property"—i.e., their slaves—into territories newly opened for settlement in the same way that northerners could bring their property.

The issue of the expansion of slavery into the territories was already a source of major political division in the country and, as was shown in Chapter 1, resulted in the creation of the Republican Party. If the Court were to strike down the Missouri Compromise, all of Stephen Douglas' championing of "popular sovereignty" in territories like Nebraska and Kansas would be for naught. Until they were admitted as states, slavery could not be kept out of the territories by law.

The Court ruled, first, that even a freed black could not be a citizen of the United States, and, second, that Congress had no power to exclude slavery from the territories. Justices Wayne, Grier, Daniel, and Campbell all filed opinions joining all or part of Taney's majority opinion. Justice Nelson opined that, since the law of Missouri said that Scott had not been freed by his journey to free states and territories, that should be the end of the matter. Justice Catron also filed an opinion giving his own reasons for the result reached by the majority. Justice McLean and Justice Curtis each wrote lengthy dissenting opinions.

Antislavery opinion in the North was outraged. Horace Greeley's *New York Tribune* said:

> The long trumpeted decision . . . having been held over from last year in order not too flagrantly to alarm and exasperate the Free States on the evening of an important presidential election . . . is entitled to just so much moral weight as would be the judgment of a majority of those congregated in any Washington bar-room.[3]

Charles Evans Hughes, himself to serve as Chief Justice from 1930 until 1941, described the Dred Scott decision as a "self-inflicted wound." Mindful of the necessity of judging the actions of people by the mores of the times in which they lived, the Court cannot be faulted only because it came out against Dred Scott. But the opinion is a strained application of legal principles prevalent in its own day.

A noted political scientist, writing more than half a century after the Dred Scott opinion, commented as follows:

> The Dred Scott decision cannot be, with accuracy, written down as a usurpation, but it can and must be written down as a gross abuse of trust by the body which rendered it. The results from that abuse of trust were, moreover, momentous.

During neither the Civil War nor the period of Reconstruction did the Supreme Court play anything like its dual role of supervision, with the result that during the one period the military powers of the President underwent undue expansion, and during the other the legislative powers of Congress. The Court itself was conscious of its weakness, yet notwithstanding its prudent disposition to remain in the background, at no time since Jefferson's first Administration has its independence been in greater jeopardy than in the decade between 1860 and 1870. So slow and laborious was its task of recuperating its shattered reputation.[4]

Time made rapid inroads on the personnel of the Court which decided the Dred Scott case. Benjamin Curtis, one of the two dissenters, resigned six months after the decision was handed down. His departure was occasioned partly by disappointment with the Court's treatment of the Dred Scott case, but also by the inadequacy of his salary as a justice. Three years later, Peter V. Daniel died; the following year John McLean died, and John Campbell resigned about the same time when his native state of Alabama seceded from the Union.

James Buchanan appointed Nathan Clifford of Maine to succeed Curtis; the result was ironic from Curtis' point of view. Clifford had served with Buchanan in the cabinet of President James Knox Polk, in which Buchanan had been Secretary of State and Clifford, Attorney General. But the nominee was known to be a "doughface"—a northerner who sympathized with the institution of slavery—and he was confirmed by a margin of only three votes in the Senate in January 1858.

Soon after his inauguration in March 1861, Abraham Lincoln had three vacancies on the Supreme Court to fill. He chose Noah Swayne, a prominent Ohio lawyer; Samuel Miller, a well-known lawyer and politician from Iowa; and David Davis, the judge before whom he used to practice in the Illinois state courts. In 1863, Congress raised the membership of the Court to ten—where it remained for only a few years—and Lincoln appointed Stephen J. Field of California to the newly created seat.

Roger Taney died in the fall of 1864, in his eighty-eighth year. Ill for much of the last few years of his life, he clung to his post because he needed the salary to support himself; Congress at that time had yet to make any provision for pensions for federal judges.

Obituaries in strongly antislavery newspapers disparaged Taney for his authorship of the Dred Scott opinion. Obituaries in Democratic newspapers eulogized him as the equal of John Marshall. The *New York Times* gave a balanced assessment:

> Had it not been for his unfortunate Dred Scott decision, all would admit that he had, through all these years, nobly sustained his high office. That decision itself, wrong as it was, did not spring from a corrupt or malignant heart. It came, we have charity to believe, from a sincere desire to compose, rather than exacerbate, sectional discord. Yet is was nonetheless an act of supreme folly, and its shadow will ever rest on his renown.[5]

Four months after Taney's death, Senator Lyman Trumbull of Illinois introduced a bill which would have placed a marble bust of Taney in the quarters used by the Supreme Court to go with the busts of John Jay, Oliver Ellsworth, and John Marshall which were already there. Charles Sumner objected "that an emancipated country should make a bust of the author of the Dred Scott decision." The debate grew heated, and the bill was eventually defeated. Nine years later, however, when Taney's successor Salmon Chase had died, a bill authorizing busts of both Chase and Taney was passed without debate.

With Taney's death, Abraham Lincoln now had the opportunity to appoint a Chief Justice. Chase, onetime Ohio Governor and senator, and until very recently Lincoln's Secretary of the Treasury, was thought to be the likely nominee. But within that year, he had committed the politically unpardonable sin of seeking to wrest the 1864 Republican presidential nomination away from Lincoln. He had attempted to use the patronage of the Treasury Department as a political machine to that end, but failed. He resigned in June 1864 over a minor patronage dispute with Lincoln, which fairly typified his character. He was egotistical to a fault—his detractors said that in his personal Trinity there were four persons rather than three—a man of marked ability but of overweening pride.

Lincoln, according to Congressman George Boutwell, said that Chase had the necessary prominence for the job, and that since he had drafted wartime legislation which was now being challenged in the courts, he would probably vote to sustain it. But, said Lincoln, there was a strong reason against the Chase appointment, and that was that he was determined to be President, and that if as Chief Justice he did not get that bee out of his bonnet, it would be bad for the Court and bad for the country. Finally, in a gesture which illustrates his magnanimity, he nominated Chase to be Chief Justice in December 1864.

Unfortunately for himself and for the Court, Chase never did give up his ambition to be President. When the Republican nominating convention showed no interest in his candidacy in 1868, he turned to the Democratic convention, where, as noted in Chapter 3, he made a good run until losing out to Horatio Seymour. In 1872, it was the same story, with Chase first having his name submitted to the Democratic convention and then to the

Liberal Republican convention meeting in Cincinnati. There his colleague, David Davis, ran up a considerable vote, but not Chase.

In contrast, when Chase's successor on the Court, Morrison R. Waite, was touted as a Republican presidential candidate in 1876, he promptly scotched the idea in a letter to his cousin, John T. Waite. In the course of the letter he observed:

> Of course, I am always grateful to my friends for their efforts in my behalf. No one ever had those more faithful or indulgent and no one ever had more cause for gratitude than I. But do you think it quite right for one, who occupies the first judicial position in the land, to permit the use of his name for a mere political office. The Presidency although high is only political. In my judgment, my predecessor detracted from his fame by permitting himself to think he wanted the Presidency. Whether true or not it was *said* that he permitted his ambitions in that direction to influence his judicial opinions. . . . I am not one of those who believe that he did so consciously, but one who occupies his position should keep himself above suspicion. . . .[6]

One of the first major cases to be decided by the Court under Chief Justice Chase was *Ex Parte Milligan,* in 1866. Members of a secret society in Indiana were charged with plotting to free Confederate prisoners of war held in Illinois and to seize the federal arsenal in Rock Island. Secretary of War Stanton decided that they should be tried before a military commission rather than before ordinary courts. They were convicted, and sought review in the Supreme Court. The majority opinion, written by the Court by Justice David Davis, held that persons who were not in the armed forces could not be tried before a military tribunal so long as the civil courts were open to hear their case. All nine justices agreed on the result in that case, but Chief Justice Chase spoke for a minority of four in criticizing the breadth of the majority opinion.

In the following year, Congress passed several Reconstruction acts, dividing the former Confederate states into military districts and abolishing the right of trial by jury for defendants charged with violating their many prohibitions. William H. McCardle, a newspaper editor in Jackson, Mississippi, was accused of having libeled the military authorities and also with having "impeded Reconstruction" by some of the pieces he had published in his newspaper. He was convicted by a military tribunal and sought review in the Supreme Court on the grounds that under the Milligan case, he, being a civilian, could not be tried before a military tribunal. The case elicited great public interest, and on the motion of McCardle's lawyer the Court granted expedited review, with arguments scheduled for March 1868.

The spring of 1868 was probably the apogee of the domination of Congress by the Radical Republicans. Andrew Johnson had been impeached by the House of Representatives in late February, and his trial would begin on March 30. If convicted, he would be removed from office, to be succeeded by the president pro tem of the Senate, Senator Ben Wade of Ohio—as radical a Republican as there was in that body.

It was in this setting that the House of Representatives by a parliamentary trick amended an obscure bill modifying the Supreme Court's appellate jurisdiction to entirely repeal the appellate jurisdiction of the Court as to appeals in habeas corpus cases such as McCardle's. The Radical Republicans did not want the Supreme Court to pass on the validity of the Reconstruction Acts.

The Court, having heard argument on the merits, now had to consider this new wrinkle in the case. It adjourned its term without reaching any decision and, the following year, acceded to the will of Congress. In a unanimous opinion by Chief Justice Chase, it held that the Constitution gave Congress plenary power to regulate the appellate jurisdiction of the Supreme Court and that the measure passed the previous year had in fact divested the Court of jurisdiction to hear the case.

One of the reasons that Abraham Lincoln had appointed Chase as Chief Justice was his belief that because Chase had played a major part in drafting what was called the Greenback Legislation he would surely vote to sustain its constitutionality as a member of the Supreme Court. In order to finance the Civil War, Congress had made paper currency—not backed up by any promise to pay gold or silver—legal tender for payment of debts. Such a move was undoubtedly desirable so far as financing the war was concerned, but its effects were felt beyond the war; debtors embraced it, and creditors resented it.

In 1867, the Court heard argument in *Hepburn v. Griswald*,[7] which was an appeal from a decision of the highest court of Kentucky upholding the constitutionality of the Legal Tender Act. Only seven of the nine justices participated in the ruling, and by a majority of 4 to 3 they ruled that the Legal Tender Act was unconstitutional. The opinion was written, much to people's amazement, by none other than Chief Justice Chase, who held that the power to make such laws was neither expressly conferred on Congress nor incident to any express power.

But at the very moment that the opinion was being handed down, President Grant nominated two additional justices to the Court—William Strong of Pennsylvania, and Joseph Bradley of New Jersey. One year later, the Court heard a second case involving the question—*Knox v. Lee*[8]—and in the spring of 1871 handed down an opinion holding that the Legal Tender Act *was,* after all, constitutional. The two new justices—Strong and Bradley—joined with the three justices who had dissented in the first case—Swayne, Miller, and Davis—to support the new ruling. The justices who were in the majority the first time—Chase, Nelson, Clifford, and Field—quite bitterly dissented.

There were public complaints that Grant had deliberately named the two new justices in order to reverse the first decision, but this is not borne out by the facts. The effect on the public was nonetheless unfavorable—a complete turnaround from one case to another within a period of two years, and the two new justices making the decisive votes in the second case to overturn the first.

Salmon P. Chase died in the spring of 1873; Grant now had the opportunity to appoint his successor. He proceeded to make a complete hash of the process, not only diminishing the office of President but that of Chief Justice as well. Grant does not deserve personal blame for much of the corruption which occurred during his eight years in office, but he did often operate on the basis of personal whim. In an effort to find a new Chief Justice, he behaved like a child playing the parlor game of pin the tail on the donkey, in which all of the participants wear blindfolds.

Grant waited for six months—from May until November, 1873—before sending up any nomination at all. He then offered the position to his staunch political ally, New York Senator Roscoe Conkling. Conkling, able and politically ambitious, declined, saying to friends, "I could not take the place for I would be forever gnawing my chains."[9]

Three sitting justices aspired to the position: Miller, a remarkably able and clear-headed man; Swayne, whose eagerness for the position quite outmatched his abilities; and Bradley, only four years on the Court. But Grant decided he would not make any "side bench" appointment (i.e., promote a sitting justice to the center chair of Chief Justice).

He then offered the position successively to two Republican senators, Oliver Morton of Indiana and Timothy Howe of Wisconsin. Both declined. Grant next went to Hamilton Fish, his Secretary of State. Fish, perhaps with undue modesty in the light of other candidates being considered, felt that his twenty years away from the practice of law would handicap him; he, too, turned down the offer. Grant then discussed with Fish a possible temporary appointment of Massachusetts lawyer Caleb Cushing, with the secret understanding on Cushing's part that he would resign before Grant's term expired. His cabinet opposed this bizarre proposal, and the President again turned elsewhere.

He nominated his Attorney General, George H. Williams, a man not highly regarded in the legal profession, who was open to charges of corruption. He had purchased an elegant landaulet (a coupé with a folding top), as well as liveries for his personal servants, from the contingent fund of the Department of Justice. He had also mingled his personal accounts with those of the department, and his wife was accused of selling immunity from prosecution. Even the President's staunchest supporters in the Senate made it clear that the nomination would be defeated, and Grant withdrew Williams' name.

By now it was early January 1874. The bar and the press intensified their criticism of his selection process. As if to defy them, he sent to the Senate the nomination of Caleb Cushing. Cushing was an able, experienced lawyer, who had served as Attorney General in the cabinet of Franklin Pierce. But he had been around the track once too often to surface as Chief Justice in 1874. He was seventy-four years old and was remembered by Republicans as a champion of the southern "fire-eater" faction of the Democratic Party immediately before the Civil War.

The final blow came when opponents uncovered a letter which he had written to Confederate President Jefferson Davis in March 1861, recommending a government clerk for employment with the Confederacy. Though harmless on its face, in post–Civil War Washington it suggested ties between Cushing and the Confederacy. The *Washington Chronicle,* a newspaper published by Justice Miller's son-in-law, Robert B. Corkhill, falsely stated that the letter referred to the applicant as an experienced worker "in the Ordnance Department at Washington," who may be "of special service to you."

A week after his nomination, Cushing requested Grant to withdraw his nomination.

At a cabinet meeting the same day, several other names surfaced, including that of Morrison R. Waite, one of the American counsel at the Alabama Claims Arbitration in Geneva. Waite was a successful lawyer from Toledo, Ohio. He had not played any major part in politics but had served as the president of the Ohio Constitutional Convention in 1872. His participation in the Alabama Claims Arbitration also stood him in good stead.

After Grant had nominated Cushing, *The Nation,* an organ of Liberal Republican opinion, said: "In the nomination of Mr. Cushing for Chief-Justice, it may be said that the President has at last entered the small circle of eminent lawyers and then with great care has chosen the worst man in it."[10]

Now Grant would venture outside that circle. Waite had supporters throughout the country all during the nomination process. Samuel L. M. Barlow, a prominent New York lawyer and a Democrat, began to urge Waite's nomination in the summer of 1873. Bancroft Davis (the U.S. minister to Germany) and Elihu B. Washburne, who became acquainted with him during the Alabama Claims Arbitration, joined in endorsing his appointment. When Grant decided against making any side-bench appointment from the Court, his Secretary of the Interior, Columbus Delano, who had favored Justice Swayne, supported his fellow Ohioan Waite. On January 19, Grant sent the nomination of Waite to be Chief Justice to the Senate. Three days later, he was unanimously confirmed. The nation was glad to have the search over:

> With a sigh of relief, Secretary of State Hamilton Fish picked up his pen and wrote, "we had" "*a time*" over the Chief Justiceship. . . . It has been a hard parturition—I hope that what has been produced may prove successful. From wise old Gideon Welles, the great diarist of the Lincoln Cabinet, came a similar sentiment. Waite, he allowed, would probably make a good judge. "It is a wonder," Welles told his son, "that Grant did not pick up some old acquaintance, who was a stage driver or bartender for the place. We may be thankful he has done so well."[11]

It was now seventeen years since the Dred Scott decision, and the Court, albeit with some setbacks—the reversal in the Legal Tender cases and the just-described Chief Justice nomination—was slowly but surely being restored to its rightful place as the head of the third branch of the federal government. The Chief Justice would add to its stature during the fourteen years during which he presided over it. But now, three years after the Waite nomination, the justices were being asked to serve as members of an electoral commission whose actions and conclusions were bound to be controversial.

As the House and Senate committees coalesced in their formulation of the Commission plan, public attention naturally focused on David Davis. Most knowledgeable observers believed that not only the congressional members of the Commission would favor the candidate of their own party, but that the four justices named to the Commission would do likewise. The identity of the fifth justice could be decisive.

Davis was born in Cecil County, Maryland, in 1815. His mother, widowed while pregnant with him, lived on her father's plantation in the northernmost part of Maryland's Eastern Shore. When the boy was five, his mother remarried and he went to live with his uncle, an Episcopal rector, in Annapolis. For the next few years, he alternated between residing with his uncle and with his mother and stepfather. At age thirteen, he was placed on a stagecoach headed to Kenyon College, in Gambier, Ohio. After graduating from Kenyon in 1832, at the age of seventeen, he began the study of law for three years with an attorney in Lenox, Massachusetts. He then migrated westward to central Illinois and purchased a law practice in Bloomington. In 1838, he married Sarah Walker, to whom he had become engaged while clerking in Lenox.

Davis, already weighing two hundred pounds, began to gain even more weight after his marriage; he would eventually weigh about three hundred pounds. In Illinois, he unsuccessfully sought the office of district attorney of the newly created Eighth District of the state court system, which comprised much of the central part of the state. He enthusiastically supported William Henry Harrison in the presidential campaign of 1840. Only twenty-five years old, he himself received the Whig nomination for state senator from his district. He campaigned on horseback but lost the election to his opponent by a small margin.

Shortly afterward, Davis grew discontented with Illinois, where the hard times prevailing throughout the nation seemed hardest of all. He talked of getting a federal appointment, or

Justice Stephen Field, 1895.

moving to St. Louis. But his law practice in the circuit courts began growing, and in 1844 he was elected as a Whig to the state legislature.

At about the same time, Davis and his partner, Wells Colton, represented an insolvent Bloomington merchant named James Allin. Colton went to Philadelphia with an offer to pay off all of Allin's creditors at the rate of 25 cents on the dollar, $1,000 in cash, and the balance by conveyance of 1,900 acres of vacant land near Bloomington. The creditors didn't want the land, but accepted the compromise on the condition that Davis and Colton take the land and execute a two-year promissory note for $1,700 to them. The partners easily repaid the note within two years, acquiring the land for less than $1 per acre. This transaction was the foundation of Davis' wealth, made by getting land cheaply in a growing state. Davis acquired other land by purchasing tax titles where owners had failed to pay their property tax.

He was a delegate to the state constitutional convention in 1847. That convention revised the geographical configuration of the state's judiciary. When this revision took place, Davis ran as a candidate for judge in the newly configured Eighth District and won handily. He would remain in that position until Lincoln appointed him to the Supreme Court in 1862. He and Lincoln had become great friends.

> With the completion of his circuit the judge had traversed an area, he informed Sarah's [his wife's] father, almost as large as the whole State of Connecticut. Travel had been rigorous, living usually miserable, but despite his complaints, he thoroughly enjoyed it. Most of his joy came from his relations with his companions, particularly Lincoln, the only lawyer except the state's attorney who traveled the entire circuit with him. Their close friendship soon became well known throughout the circuit.[12]

Davis warmly supported Lincoln in his losing senatorial campaign against Stephen A. Douglas in 1858. Then both he and Lincoln began looking to the Republican presidential nomination in 1860. The Republican convention convened in the Wigwam in Chicago in May 1860. Davis went to the city several days ahead of time and discovered that all of the candidates except Lincoln—William H. Seward of New York, Salmon P. Chase of Ohio, Edward Bates of Missouri, and Simon Cameron of Pennsylvania—had established headquarters. He rented two rooms in the Tremont Hotel at his own expense and became Lincoln's de facto manager.

Seward, by virtue of his seniority, was the preconvention favorite. Twenty years earlier he had served two terms as Governor of New York, the most populous state in the union. He had gone on to represent that state in the Senate from 1848 until the present. But many of the party faithful thought he was too close to the abolitionist wing of the party to be elected. The Indiana and Pennsylvania delegations were firmly opposed to him. If he became the candidate, they said, the party could not carry their own state elections, which were held in October rather than November.

Davis' strategy was to antagonize no delegates and to secure from delegations committed to other candidates a promise of support for Lincoln on a second ballot. Lincoln had instructed Davis to make no binding pledges in order to obtain delegates, but he was in Springfield and Davis and his cohorts were in the heat of the Chicago battle. The leader of the Pennsylvania delegation demanded that Simon Cameron, the corrupt party boss of that state, be Lincoln's Secretary of the Treasury, and that Cameron have sole control of federal patronage in the state. Davis promised that Pennsylvania would have a place in the cabinet but balked at going further. The issue was finally negotiated, and Pennsylvania committed to Lincoln on the second ballot.

On the first ballot, Seward had 173½ votes (some states sent sixty delegates, so each had half a vote), Lincoln 102 votes, with the rest scattered. On the second ballot, Lincoln rose to 181, while Seward gained only ten to reach 184½. On the third ballot,

Lincoln bested Seward by a vote of 231½ to 180. He was only 1½ votes short of the absolute majority required for the nomination. These votes were given to him by four Ohio delegates who switched from Chase to Lincoln. Pandemonium broke out in the Wigwam, and Davis broke into tears. He immediately telegraphed Lincoln:

> DON'T COME HERE FOR GOD'S SAKE. YOU WILL BE TELEGRAPHED BY OTHERS TO COME. IT IS THE UNITED ADVICE OF YOUR FRIENDS NOT TO COME. THIS IS IMPORTANT.[13]

Davis wanted Lincoln to learn from others of the commitments made to secure his nomination.

Even before Lincoln was inaugurated in March 1861, he was besieged by office-seekers. Among the offices which he had to fill were three Supreme Court vacancies. He nominated Swayne of Ohio and Miller of Iowa to two of them. But what about his home state of Illinois? Surely there was no one to whom Lincoln was more indebted for his presidency than Davis. And in October 1862, he appointed Davis to the Supreme Court. Davis went to Washington to be sworn in, not without misgivings. He confided to William Orme, a young lawyer from Bloomington:

> I often doubt, Orme, whether I could sustain myself on the Supreme Bench.... I certainly could not without hard study.... I have but little legal learning.[14]

These misgivings persisted even as he was about to attend the first session of the Court's new term. Sarah had remained in Bloomington, and he expressed his feelings to her:

If I had felt in Illinois, as I have this week, I never would have come to Washington. . . . What strikes everybody as the highest good fortune, has been to me like ashes. . . . I will try the judgeship and if it don't suit me, or if I don't suit it, I will resign.[15]

On December 10, Davis took his seat at the extreme left of the bench in the Capitol. The Court's term began on that day, and usually ran until some time in April. For the rest of the year, Davis would sit as a trial judge in Illinois and Indiana.

The basic work of the Supreme Court at that time was quite different than what it is today. Now there are federal courts of appeals in twelve different geographic regions, and a litigant who loses at the trial level must go first to the court of appeals; if he loses there, he may then petition the Supreme Court for review. But the odds against success in this latter endeavor are overwhelming. Of the many thousands of petitions for review each term, the Court customarily grants fewer than one hundred. The votes of four of the nine justices are required in order to grant review, and this practice limits the Court's decisions to cases of truly national importance.

But in Davis' time, there were no federal courts of appeals, and one who lost in the trial court could appeal directly to the Supreme Court. And the Court had no discretion to decline to hear an appeal; it was required to decide every case brought to it. So while the Court then did on occasion review a case of great national importance—Davis would write the opinion in such a case four years hence*—such cases were few and far between. The staple of judicial business was cases that were brought into federal court only because the plaintiff and defendant were citi-

*The Milligan case, more fully described on pages 126–27.

zens of two different states. There was no need for any sort of federal legal question to be decided. The result was that the justices spent most of their time on cases which involved property or contract law of a particular state, with no consequences except for the parties themselves.

Davis would repeatedly vow to confine himself to his judicial work. But he was a politician at heart, and frequently intervened, not only with Lincoln, but with various government departments, to obtain clerkships or military promotions for the son of a friend, or the son of a friend of a friend. He wore out his welcome with Lincoln, and complained that Lincoln did not seek his advice on any subject. When Sarah chided him on his absence from home, he replied:

> I cannot resign my office now until I have satisfied the public mind that I am competent to discharge its duties. When I have done that, I am perfectly willing to resign and live quietly with you and my children in Illinois.[16]

After Lincoln was assassinated in April 1865, Davis was appointed administrator of his estate by an Illinois court and took on the extrajudicial duty of dealing with Lincoln's wife Mary—not an easy task. During the two years he held this position, he increased the value of the estate by prudent investments, and when it was wound up he refused to take any part of the customary administrator's fees.

In March 1866, the Milligan case was argued to the Supreme Court. Davis' opinion for the majority pleased the Democrats but displeased the radical element in the Republican Party. The *Washington Chronicle* proclaimed that "the friends of traitors will be glad that treason, once vanquished upon the battle field and hunted from every other retreat, has at last found a shelter in the bosom of the Supreme Court." The *Philadelphia North American* pointed out the common last name of the writer of the Court's opinion and the President of the Confederacy. Davis, never completely self-assured of his ability as a judge, was hurt by these criticisms. But he held firmly to his view that the opinion was correct, saying:

> This Court would be a hell on earth to me unless I can decide questions according to the light which God has given me. I hope that God will give me strength to utter my convictions and never to quail before any political tempest.[17]

The radical attack on his Milligan opinion, together with his dissatisfaction with that element's determination to impeach and convict President Andrew Johnson, caused Davis to gradually abandon allegiance to the Republican Party. But he regarded the Democratic Party as still tainted by its association with secession. He found little satisfaction in the day-to-day work of the Court:

> I write the shortest opinions of anyone on the bench. If I had to . . . write legal essays as some judges do, I would quit the concern.[18]

The ground was now ready for the presidential seed to be planted, and in 1871 a group of Illinois legislators urged him to run for President. He thanked them but said he was not interested. But support for his candidacy began to grow. In early 1872, the call went out for a convention of Liberal Republicans—anti-Grant—to meet in Cincinnati, as described in Chapter 1. Davis was regarded as a front-runner for this nomination until the eleventh hour, when the cabal of newspaper publishers decided to prevent his nomination. The nomination, of course, went to Horace Greeley, and Davis voted for Greeley.

By the time Morrison Waite became Chief Justice in 1874, Davis was sixty years old and not in robust health. The Court's term, originally less than five months long, now stretched out for more than seven months to accommodate its greatly increased docket. He almost decided to resign, but was persuaded by friends to at least wait until Grant was no longer President.

So one might say that the congressional drafters of the Commission bill had some warning of the fact that Davis would not long remain on the Court. But in order to serve the purposes of the bill, he didn't need to remain indefinitely; the Commission's work would surely be finished by March 4, the last day of Grant's presidency.

At the very time the Electoral Commission bill was moving through Congress, however, the Illinois legislature met to elect a United States senator from that state. The term of Republican incumbent John A. Logan had expired. He sought reelection and was opposed by Democrat John M. Palmer. The Democrats and Republicans in the joint session of the Illinois legislature were almost evenly divided, and the balance of power was held by a small group of Independents. This group, together with the Democrats, gave Davis a few votes in the early balloting, but for a number of ballots after that he received no votes. Then on the thirty-fifth ballot—a week into the session—the same group of Independents and Democrats gave Davis ninety-seven votes— just short of the number needed for election. The following day, he received the necessary additional votes and was elected senator.

Davis knew of the balloting in Illinois but thought he had been eliminated early in the race and was surprised at his election. Yet it fit in perfectly with his plans; he need not look for another job after March 4, 1877. He could still, of course, serve on the Commission, since his senatorial term would not begin until March 4, but in spite of the pleas of the democratically inclined justices named to the Commission, he declined to do so. They would have to find another justice, but another with Davis' independent status was unavailable. All of the remaining members had been appointed by Republican presidents.

— CHAPTER 7 —

THE MOST SENIOR of the justices designated by name in the law creating the Electoral Commission was Nathan Clifford of Maine. He was a loyal Democrat, steeped in the tradition of Jacksonian democracy. He held high public office in the days of the Democratic ascendancy before the Civil War and was something of an anachronism afterward.

Clifford was born in the village of Rumney, New Hampshire, in 1803. He turned to the study of law, was admitted to the bar, and then moved to Newfield, Maine, to begin his practice and was soon elected as a Democratic delegate to the lower house of the Maine legislature.

He was a large man, in robust health, and willing to work hard. He was selected Speaker for two of his last three terms in that body, and served as a delegate to the Democratic National Convention in Baltimore in 1832. Two years later he was appointed attorney general of Maine, and in 1838 was elected to Congress. He served two terms there before a redistricting deprived him of another term. But when James K. Polk was elected President in 1844, he named Clifford as his Attorney General.

Senator Roscoe Conkling, c. 1860s.

Clifford was called upon by Polk to handle delicate negotiations concerning the conduct of the Mexican War. Polk and his Secretary of State, James Buchanan, disagreed over the conduct of that conflict, and Clifford served as an intermediary between them. After the United States forces had won, Nicholas Trist, the American commissioner, negotiated a treaty with Mexico to conclude the war. But when it was presented to the United States Senate, that body proceeded to amend the treaty. Clifford was one of the emissaries sent by Polk to Mexico to persuade the Mexican authorities to accept the amendments. He remained in Mexico as minister plenipotentiary to that country until Zachary Taylor succeeded Polk as President in 1849.

Clifford then returned to the practice of law in Portland, Maine, and though he argued at least one case before the United States Supreme Court, his work did not bring him financial independence. When in 1857 the New England seat on the Supreme Court became vacant upon the resignation of Benjamin Curtis, Buchanan quite naturally turned to his former colleague in the Polk administration to fill it. Clifford's nomination brought forth considerable protests from northern antislavery advocates. Though a New Englander, he was known as a dough-face, a northerner with southern sympathies.

The *New York Evening Post* (January 14–15, 1858) commented:

> Mr. Clifford owes his appointment exclusively to his party associations, unsupported by the wishes or recommendation of the bar of his circuit. His sympathies coincide entirely with those which the Court have manifested, and bring the strength of his vote to the sectional action of the Court, without any independence or great legal ability.

On January 12, 1858, the Senate confirmed him by the narrow margin of 26 to 23. The narrowness of the margin showed that the repercussions from the Kansas–Nebraska Act were already dividing the Democratic Party. Every senator from the eleven states which would later secede voted to confirm Clifford, but only four voted that way from the remaining states.

Nathan Clifford would serve twenty-three years on the Court, writing more than his share of the Court's opinions in that time. But he authored none of that body's important constitutional opinions, specializing instead in the fields of maritime and commercial law and Mexican land grants. He would remain a Democrat, forgoing an opportunity to retire in hopes that a Democratic President would be able to name his successor. Even when incapacitated by a stroke in 1880, he refused to resign. He lingered on as an invalid until his death in the summer of 1881.

THE SECOND of the two Democrats designated in the Electoral Commission law was Stephen J. Field of California. He was a man of unusual ability, well respected by the bar for his work on the supreme court of California at the time of his appointment to the United States Supreme Court. Modesty, however, was not one of his prominent traits. He coupled with his ability and legal knowledge a determination to see his views prevail, a quality which made him one of the most influential justices of his time. But this characteristic also had its negative side; he would pursue personal disputes to the point of vindictiveness and would act as a judge in a manner which was debatable even by the looser ethical standards of his own day. His experience in the gold-rush days of California, a true chapter of the "wild, wild west"—makes his life more interesting than that of a typical Supreme Court justice.

Field's biographer, Carl J. Swisher, describes his appearance at the time he took his seat on the Supreme Court:

> He was a trimly built man of forty-seven years. Curly, dark brown hair covered his unusually large head, save for a bald spot at the top; and a beard of the same color adorned his

chin. Piercing, blue-gray eyes looked out from under heavy brows, eyes which suggested something of the alertness of the brain which lay behind them. His demeanor was that of a solemn, judicial poise.[1]

Stephen Field was born in Haddam, Connecticut, in 1816. His was a talented family: he would become a justice of the Supreme Court of the United States, his brother David Dudley Field would become a nationally known New York lawyer and politician, and his brother Cyrus Field would lay the trans-atlantic cable in 1866.

Stephen Field attended Williams College for four years, then went to New York to study law in the office of his brother David. He became a junior partner with his brother and practiced there from 1841 until 1848. In 1849, word of the discovery of gold in California at Sutter's Mill lured him, along with thousands of others, to the goldfields.

There were only two ways to go there from the East Coast, since there was not yet any transcontinental railroad. One could take a ship around Cape Horn and sail back up the Pacific to San Francisco, or one could take a ship to the Isthmus of Panama, cross the isthmus, and take another ship from the Pacific side up to San Francisco. Field chose the latter route, and after contracting cholera in Panama, he finally sailed through the Golden Gate in late December 1849.

San Francisco was crowded with men newly arrived from all over the world. After a few days in the city, Field took a river-boat up the Sacramento River to the newly established city of Marysville, where he was immediately elected alcalde—an office in the Spanish system of government which corresponded roughly to justice of the peace.

Field was displaced the following year with the arrival of a district judge, William R. Turner, who was appointed under the newly adopted California constitution. Field and Turner had a series of run-ins, resulting in Field's being cited for contempt and fined a substantial amount of money. Field had his revenge when he drafted a bill which rearranged the state judicial districts so that Turner was transferred to the far northern wilderness of Trinity and Klamath Counties. It was perhaps the first, but certainly not the last, of the personal feuds which dogged him.

He built a very successful law practice in Marysville, and appeared as counsel in the California Supreme Court on sixty different occasions. He became a leader of the state bar, with an annual income of over $40,000, but was not satisfied with his position. In 1857, he was elected to the California Supreme Court, giving up his lucrative practice for a state salary of $6,000 per year. He joined with Justice Peter Burnett and Justice David Terry on that court. Terry had come on the court two years earlier and was possessed of a fiery temper. He resigned from the bench two years later and thereupon challenged United States Senator David C. Broderick to a duel. Broderick was killed. Terry's temper would come back to haunt Field many years later.

Field sat on the supreme court of California for six years and was its recognized leader at a time when it handed down formative decisions in the law of the state. When Congress created a Tenth Circuit, and a tenth seat on the Supreme Court in 1863, the bar of the Pacific coast supported him for the appointment. His brother David Dudley Field had played a part in the organization of the Republican Party and in the nomination of Lincoln as its candidate for President in 1860. When another old friend of Lincoln's went to him to urge Field's appointment, the President agreed that Field was a fit candidate and asked only,

"Does David want his brother to have it?" "Yes," said the other. "Then he shall have it" was the instant reply, and the nomination was sent in that afternoon and confirmed by the Senate unanimously.[2]

During the thirty-four years he served on the nation's high court, Field became a champion of property rights. The first major cases to come before the Court involving the Fourteenth Amendment, enacted after the Civil War, were known as the Slaughterhouse Cases. In 1869, a corrupt Louisiana legislature passed a law prohibiting the slaughter of animals throughout greater New Orleans except in the facility of one particular corporation. The other butchers in the city sued, claiming that they were denied their right to engage in a legitimate business. They relied on a provision of the Fourteenth Amendment which forbade a state to deprive any person of the "privileges and immunities" of citizens of the United States.

The Court divided 5 to 4 on the question, with Justice Miller speaking for the majority which denied relief to the butchers. He observed that the amendment had been adopted for the benefit of the newly freed slaves and not for rival businessmen. Justice Field wrote an impassioned dissent, saying that the Amendment secured to everyone their "common right" as citizens. Field's expansive view did not prevail in this case, but eventually it would become embedded in the Court's Fourteenth Amendment jurisprudence through another provision of that amendment.

Field, like his colleagues, was required to sit as a circuit judge—he in California—for a part of the time that the Supreme Court was not in session in Washington. It was this duty which led to a fateful encounter with David Terry. William Sharon, a mining tycoon and senator from Nevada, conducted an amorous affair with a much younger woman, Sarah Hill. When it broke up, she claimed that they had secretly entered into a marriage contract, and sued in state court asking for divorce, alimony, and a part of Sharon's property. Sharon brought his own lawsuit in federal court, seeking to cancel the purported marriage contract as a fraud and a forgery.

Throughout protracted deposition hearings in the federal case, Sarah Hill became abusive and threatened to shoot one of the opposing lawyers. Sharon's counsel appealed to the circuit court to restrain her. Field sat with another circuit judge, Lorenzo Sawyer, who was hearing the principal case, and they ordered the marshal to search Sarah Hill for weapons whenever she appeared at a deposition.

The circuit court ruled against Hill on the merits of her case later, but meanwhile Sharon had died and David Terry had become the attorney for Sarah Hill. Two weeks after the adverse decision of the circuit court, they were married. In a later proceeding in the same case, Hill, accompanied by Terry, became violent in the courtroom and had to be restrained over Terry's strong objection. Hill immediately afterward threatened to kill Field. Terry and Hill were both held in contempt of court.

Field returned to Washington after this imbroglio, and the next summer he was urged by friends in California not to return to the state then because of the uproar created by these proceedings. Field was determined to do so, however, saying:

> I cannot and will not allow threats of personal violence to deter me from the regular performance of my judicial duties at the times and places fixed by law. As a judge of the highest court in the country, I should be ashamed to look any man in the face if I allowed a ruffian, by threats against

my person, to keep me from holding the regular courts in my circuit.[3]

A marshal named David Neagle was deputized to travel with Field in California in order to protect him. In mid-August 1889, Field was traveling by train from Los Angeles to San Francisco; he and Neagle both had berths in the same sleeping car. When the train reached Fresno, Neagle saw that the Terrys boarded, and told Field. The train later stopped at Lathrop to allow passengers to get breakfast. Field and Neagle walked into the station dining room and sat down. Shortly afterward, David and Sarah Terry walked in, but Sarah left immediately while Terry took a seat at another table. What followed is described by Swisher in these words:

> Terry remained seated for a time and then got up and walked down the aisle toward the door, this time taking the aisle immediately behind Field. Those who were watching him assumed that he was going to join his wife. When he arrived at a point just behind Field he turned suddenly and struck him twice on the side of the face or head. Succeeding events came too quickly for accurate observation. Neagle leaped to his feet and shouted "stop, stop!" Neagle saw a terrible expression on the face of Terry, and thought that the latter reached for his knife. With his right hand extended Neagle drew his gun with his left and fired twice in rapid succession, killing Terry instantly.[4]

A county sheriff arrested Neagle, over Field's protest, and took him to the county jail in Stockton. Efforts were made to arrest Field as he proceeded alone to San Francisco, but

U.S. Marshals foiled them, and Field arrived safely in San Francisco. Word of Terry's shooting made headlines across the country. Neagle was charged with murder in state court, and his attorneys sought a writ of habeas corpus from the federal court in San Francisco.

The circuit court granted the writ, and the state authorities—who wished to try Neagle for murder in the state court—appealed to the U.S. Supreme Court. The law governing the use of the writ in federal courts provided that it could be obtained for a person in custody "for any act done or omitted in pursuance of a law of the United States." The state parties said that no "law of the United States" authorized the appointment of Neagle to guard Field while he performed his judicial duties on circuit in California. The Supreme Court, in an opinion written by Justice Miller less than a month before his death, held that even though there was no act of Congress authorizing Neagle's appointment, the circuit court had nonetheless been correct in its decision. Miller's opinion said:

> . . . in the protection of the person and the life of Mr. Justice Field while in the discharge of his official duties, Neagle was authorized to resist the attack of Terry upon him; that Neagle was correct in the belief that without prompt action on his part the assault of Terry upon the judge would have ended in the death of the latter; that such being his well-founded belief, he was justified in taking the life of Terry, as the only means of preventing the death of the man who was intended to be his victim; that in taking the life of Terry, under the circumstances, he was acting under the authority of the law of the United States, and was justified in so doing. . . .[5]

Neagle was thereupon set free.

. . .

SAMUEL FREEMAN MILLER was the senior of the two Republican justices named to the Electoral Commission. He was appointed to the Court by Lincoln in 1862 and served until his death in 1890. Both by reason of ability and length of service, he ranked with Field in his influence on the development of constitutional law, though the two were often of opposite views. Carl

Ulysses S. Grant, c. 1872.

Brent Swisher, Field's biographer, describes Miller in these words:

> Justice Miller, who was a colleague of Justice Field's for more than a quarter of a century, may be taken as sharply in contrast with him in appearance, disposition, and habit. He was a great, stocky man, heavy of build and heavy of tread. He was square faced and smooth shaven. People sought his company because he rarely failed to have a good time, and in enjoying himself he radiated mirth and happiness to others.[6]

Miller was born in 1816—in the same year as Field—in Richmond, Kentucky, the first of eight children. He studied medicine at Transylvania University in nearby Lexington. Upon receiving his degree at the age of twenty-two, he took up residence in Barbourville in southeastern Kentucky. Becoming dissatisfied with the practice of medicine after a few years, he began studying law in his spare time and was eventually admitted to the Kentucky bar. Politically, he was a Whig and sought to advance the cause of gradual emancipation in Kentucky. Failing in this, he and his family moved to Keokuk, Iowa, a city on the Mississippi River in the southeastern corner of that state.

There he entered into a partnership with one of the town's leading lawyers and in a short time became a highly respected lawyer in his own right. He was active in Republican politics from the time of the party's infancy and served as a member of the state's central committee. He campaigned actively for Lincoln in 1860, and the state went Republican by a wide margin.

As already noted, when Lincoln took office, he had three vacancies in the Supreme Court to fill. He did not act immediately, because Congress was in the process of realigning the federal judicial circuits. After much deliberation, Iowa was grouped along with Missouri, Kansas, and Minnesota in a Trans-Mississippi Circuit. The Iowa bar, and its congressional delegation, enthusiastically supported Miller's candidacy for one of the vacancies. Lincoln nominated him in July 1862, and the Senate confirmed him in half an hour without reference to a committee.

Miller would serve on the Court for nearly three decades, very likely the dominant figure during that time. He would write twice his share of opinions in cases involving constitutional questions. One of the best known was in the Slaughterhouse Cases (described on page 149). His opinion placed a narrow construction on the portion of the amendment before the Court, and went on to comment that its intent was only to benefit the newly freed slaves. Field, joined by three others, dissented, insisting that it should receive a much broader construction. In the long run it was Field's view, not Miller's, which prevailed.

When the chief justiceship became vacant upon Salmon Chase's death in 1873, Miller was the candidate most widely endorsed by the nation's bar. Typical is the comment of the *Albany Law Journal:*

> We know of no one in the country whose appointment would be so appropriate, or give such universal satisfaction, as would that of Mr. Justice Miller. Endowed with every moral as well as intellectual attribute which can adorn the highest judicial character, in the maturity of life, with great experience upon the bench, he would make a worthy successor of Marshall, or Taney, and of Chase.[7]

Grant, however, as described in Chapter 6, chose to look outside the Court, and Morrison Waite became Chief Justice in 1874. That summer, Miller wrote in a letter to his brother-in-law of an apparent rift between him and Justice Joseph Bradley arising out of their aspirations for the office. But the strain between them vanished with the appointment of Waite, and Miller would shortly afterward appraise Bradley: "with some allowance for eccentricity he is a useful and valuable man on the bench."[8] Bradley would be the fifth justice chosen for the Electoral Commission.

Miller's biographer, Charles Fairman, observes that "when Justice Miller died it was generally remarked that the Court had lost the ablest of its members and the greatest figure in constitutional law since Marshall." John Dillon, a widely respected circuit judge who sat frequently with Miller on circuit, was more poetic, hailing him as "easily . . . the master of us all. His frame, features and majestic port duly put in marble might stand for those of a Roman Caesar in Rome's best day; and Rome, so distinguished for its legal genius, never produced a jurisconsult more worthy of perpetual honor than . . . Justice Miller.[9]

WILLIAM STRONG of Pennsylvania was the fourth justice named to the Electoral Commission by the law creating it. The earlier drafts of the bill had not named him, but Noah Swayne, as the second Republican appointee to serve on the Commission. But, whether for reasons of geographic diversity, or, as suggested by the *New York Sun* (Wednesday, January 31, 1877), because of Swayne's expressed desire to avoid serving, is not clear.

Strong was appointed to the Court in 1870 by President Grant. Along with Bradley, who was selected at the same time, he had joined the majority opinion in *Knox v. Lee,* overruling the earlier decision in the Legal Tender cases. As a justice of the supreme court of Pennsylvania, Strong had joined an opinion of that court upholding the validity of the Greenback Laws, so his vote in *Knox v. Lee* scarcely came as a surprise. Strong was born in Connecticut in 1808 and attended Yale College before studying law. He was admitted to the Pennsylvania bar at the age of twenty-four, and proceeded to establish a successful practice in Reading. A Democrat, twice elected as a representative in Congress, in 1857 he was elected to a fifteen-year term on the Pennsylvania Supreme Court. He served there until his resignation in 1868.

Though he would stay only ten years on the U.S. Supreme Court, he wrote the opinion of the Court in several significant cases. In *Strauder v. West Virginia,*[10] for example, he spoke for the Court in holding that the Fourteenth Amendment prohibited discrimination on the basis of race in the selection of grand jurors by the states.

He resigned from the Court in 1880 but would live for another fifteen years. He remained active in the Presbyterian Church and served as president of the American Sunday School Union and of the American Tract Society.

The four justices named in the Act as members of the Electoral Commission met in Washington on Tuesday, January 30, to consider who the fifth member should be. The *New York Sun* carried this account of their deliberations:

THE CHOICE OF THE JUDGES

THREE OF THE FOUR FAVORING THE SELECTION OF DAVIS

MR. CLIFFORD VIEWING JUDGE DAVIS'S ELECTION TO THE SENATE AS A FITTING QUALIFICATION FOR THE DUTIES OF THE ELECTORAL COMMISSION

WASHINGTON. Jan. 30.—The four Justices of the Supreme Court—Messrs. Clifford, Miller, Field and Strong—whose duty it is under the Electoral bill, to select the fifth Justice, and thus complete the Grand Commission, met this morning and had a conference of several hours duration. No vote was taken, the time was simply consumed in a friendly discussion of the propriety of selecting Justice Davis as the fifth judge. It is understood that it was agreed that Justice Swayne was not to be considered available, inasmuch as he had indicated his aversion to serving on the Commission. This determination of Justice Swayne was known to be founded partly on his disinclination to assume the great labor which this new duty would impose, and partly on account of his long and close intimacy with both Mr. Tilden and Mr. Hayes. As Mr. Davis had also expressed his unwillingness to serve, it was supposed that the four judges would feel constrained to select either Justice Bradley or Justice Hunt as the fifth judge. When they came to consult this morning, however, it appeared that Messrs. Clifford, Field, and Strong were of the opinion that Mr. Davis was, of all the Justices, more eminently qualified than any member of the Court to give satisfaction to both parties in this contest. Mr. Justice Miller contended that Mr. Davis's election to the United States Senate had to some extent disqualified him; therefore he thought it would be more satisfactory to select either Mr. Hunt or Mr. Bradley. Mr. Miller's choice seemed to be Mr. Hunt, and, so far as Mr. Strong indicated a preference between these two, it was for Mr. Bradley.

Mr. Clifford indicated his entire willingness to accept Mr. Bradley as the fifth judge, but he argued that instead of

Mr. Davis's election to the Senate disqualifying him, it really made him the more eminently fit for the position. . . .

Judge Strong agreed fully with Judge Clifford, but he doubted whether Mr. Davis could be induced to reconsider his determination not to accept the position. It was, however, agreed that Judge Davis should be notified that he was the choice of three of the judges, and that they had determined to give him until tomorrow morning to reconsider.[11]

The next day, the *Sun* carried the following story on its page 1:

As foreshadowed yesterday, the election of Justice Bradley to be the fifth member of the Judicial Branch of the tripartite Electoral Commission was made very promptly and with entire unanimity, soon after the four Justices assembled this morning.

Justice Davis last night received over 50 telegrams urging him to reconsider his refusal to allow himself to be voted for as a member of the Commission, and was also called upon by a number of his friends in this city for the same purpose. He, however, replied that if he should consent to occupy that position he would consider himself necessitated to decline the Illinois Senatorship which he was not inclined to do.

In that same edition, the *Sun* expressed its editorial view of this result:

The almost absolute decision of the Presidential question is left to Judge Joseph B. Bradley of Newark, a partisan to whom his party never looked in vain. HAYES being counted in, the frauds by which this result is established will be covered with the quasi-mantle of the Supreme Court. . . .

BRADLEY WAS, INDEED, being placed in an almost impossible position. David Davis by 1877 was recognized as a genuine Independent, appointed to the Supreme Court by Lincoln, but no more sympathetic to the Republican Party than to the Democratic Party. This fact made the whole idea of an Electoral Commission palatable to many members of Congress. But now, instead of a recognized Independent, the fifth justice on the Commission was a Republican appointee who, if not deserving the condemnation in the above editorial of the *Sun,* was not thought of by anyone as an "Independent" in the same sense as Davis was.

It was said of Joseph P. Bradley that he had the face of an Italian cardinal. Appointed to the Supreme Court by Grant in 1870, he served until his death in 1892. He ranked with Miller and Field as one of the most influential justices during this period.

He was born in 1813 in upstate New York, a few miles west of Albany. His parents were married when they were seventeen, and he was the eldest of their twelve children. His birthplace was not far from that of Samuel Tilden, but his family circumstances were far more straitened. Subsistence farming was the way the Bradleys made their living. Their eldest son was educated in country schools and picked up extra knowledge from family members as he could. In his eighteenth year, he felt the need for a better education:

> Whilst my father and I were threshing out the buckwheat crop one day the desire for an education became so strong that I broke out in a way I had never done before to my poor

father. I told him that my life was being wasted . . . that I felt that I *must* have an education. He said, "I cannot afford to give you an education." I said, I did not expect him to do it, but if he would let me go (I was then over 18) I would some-how obtain an education myself; and I would fully make up to him the loss of my unexpired time before coming of age. . . .[12]

Bradley spent a year being tutored in preparation for college. To attend Rutgers College in New Brunswick, New Jersey, he walked the entire distance from Albany to New Brunswick, where he appeared in class in a homespun suit made by his mother. He distinguished himself in college, graduating in only three years. Along with two of his classmates—Frederick T. Frelinghuysen, a future senator from New Jersey, and Cortland Parker, a future president of the American Bar Association, he read law in the Newark office of Frelinghuysen's uncle. In 1839 he was admitted to practice law in New Jersey.

He decided to remain in Newark, where he was offered a partnership by the attorney for the New Jersey Railroad. Soon he came to be noticed by other railroads, and especially the Camden & Amboy. This railroad bisected the state from northeast to southwest and gained a transportation monopoly in the state. Since the docile New Jersey legislature would do nothing to reg-ulate it, the railroad's opponents sought help from Congress. Bradley defended the railroad and its activities before Congress and in the courts. He was a "railroad lawyer," and an able one.

He had an extensive practice in the federal courts and argued half a dozen cases before the Supreme Court. In one of them, *Murray v. Hoboken Land Co.,*[13] the Court gave its first exposition of the meaning of the Due Process Clause of the Fifth Amend-ment. In 1844, he married Mary Hornblower, the daughter of the Chief Justice of New Jersey. He was identified with the Republican Party and in 1862 ran unsuccessfully for Congress on that party's ticket.

The Senate confirmed his nomination to the Supreme Court with only a few dissenting votes. He and William Strong, appointed at the same time, joined with those who had dissented in the first Legal Tender case, *Hepburn v. Griswald,* to overrule that decision in the later case of *Knox v. Lee.* He joined Field's dissent in the Slaughterhouse Cases, and in 1883 would author the Court's landmark decision in the Civil Rights Cases.[14] His participation as the decisive fifteenth member of the Electoral Commission would subject him to largely undeserved opprobrium.

— CHAPTER 8 —

I N ADDITION to the five justices on the Commission, the Electoral Commission Act provided that there should be five senators and five representatives. The Senate chose Frederick Frelinghuysen of New Jersey, Oliver Morton of Indiana, and George Edmunds of Vermont, all Republicans. Allen Thurman of Ohio and Thomas Bayard of Delaware, Democrats, were also included. The House named Henry Payne of Ohio, Eppa Hunton of Virginia, and Josiah Abbott of Massachusetts, Democrats, and James Garfield of Ohio and George J. Hoar of Massachusetts, Republicans. With the naming of Joseph Bradley as the fifth justice, the membership of the Commission was now complete.

The Electoral Commission Law was just one part in the process of counting the electoral vote. First, the President of the Senate would open the certificates from each state, as provided in the Twelfth Amendment to the Constitution. If a senator or representative from a certain state objected to the certificate from that state, the question would be referred to the Commission. The Commission would then consider the matter and report back its decision to Congress. The decision of the Commission was to be final, unless overridden by a majority in each House. In practice this procedure guaranteed that the Commission's decision would be final in fact, because the Democrats had a majority in the House, and the Republicans a majority in the Senate. In the politically charged atmosphere of the time, it was inconceivable that both houses would agree to override the Commission no matter which way it decided.

That body held its first meeting on January 31, 1877, in the Supreme Court chamber (then in the Capitol building). But because its members were too numerous to fit in the justices' nine seats behind the bench, a table was set up in the middle of the courtroom. On one side sat the five justices, and the senators and representatives were arrayed around the other three sides. Justice Clifford was sworn in as president of the Commission at 11 a.m., and he then administered the oath to the other members. Representative Garfield kept a personal diary of the proceedings. This is the only contemporary source shedding light on the deliberations because they were closed to the public. At the first meeting, "one of the judges told Garfield that there had been a long struggle to decide the fifth Justice," and on the way home Justice Strong told him, "All the judges except one were very sorry to be called to the Commission."[1]

The following day the two houses of Congress met in joint session to count the electoral votes. Thomas Ferry, the President of the Senate, opened the certificates from each state, beginning with Alabama. He then handed the certificate to a teller, who announced the result shown by the certificate. The count proceeded routinely until Ferry opened not one, but three, certificates from Florida, and there were objections to all three. Democrats objected to the certificate giving Hayes the state's vote, and Republicans objected to the certificates giving it to

Tilden. The matter was accordingly referred to the Electoral Commission.

The rules of the Commission adopted at its first meeting illustrate the hybrid nature of that body; it was a creature of Congress, but it also had to decide what were at bottom questions of law. Thus the rules provided that the objectors in the joint session—who in effect were all House members—should have two hours each to present their objections. At that point, counsel for both sides would take over and presumably argue the merits of the various claims. Two hours apiece would be allotted for these presentations. Garfield wrote in his diary that the Commission had allowed too much time for argument, but this was an era of lengthy arguments. Important cases before the Supreme Court then were often argued for days at a time, whereas today each side is allowed one-half hour.

It was not entirely clear how the roles of the objectors—who had made the objections in the joint session of Congress—and of counsel before the Commission differed, if they differed at all. David Dudley Field, in Lincoln's time a Republican but now a Democratic representative from New York, led off for the Democratic objectors. He devoted considerable time to discussing the returns from only one county in Florida—Baker County in the northeastern portion of the state. He used this county, he said, as an illustration of what went on not only there but in other counties. He pointed out various procedural irregularities in the canvassing of the county's vote, then referred to the majority report of the House committee which had concluded that Tilden had won the electoral votes, and offered to prove "by a cloud of witnesses and by a host of documents" that Tilden had achieved a majority in Florida. Congressman John Randolph Tucker of Virginia joined Field's plea to the Commission to go beyond the certificates presented to the President of the Senate and examine outside evidence.

Representatives John Kasson and George McCrary urged the Republican objections to the Florida certificates which purported to give the state's electoral votes to Tilden. Kasson said that the Constitution left only a small part of the presidential electoral process to the federal government. The joint session of Congress was to count the electoral votes, but it had no authority to go behind the state's certificate. A contrary approach, he said, would "launch yourselves into a tumultuous sea of allegations of fraud, irregularity and bad motive."[2]

McCrary stressed that the Constitution itself prescribed the day when the electors in each state should cast their vote, thus making it the same throughout the nation. If it remained open to a court in a state to review the choice of electors after this date, the plan of the Constitution was defeated. And, he said, if courts in one state may do it, at the behest of one party, courts in another state may do it at the behest of the other party.

When the congressional members' time on each side had expired, counsel began their presentation. They were to discuss the merits of the question, but of course this phrase could mean different things to different people. Could the Commission "go behind" the certificates sent to the President of the Senate and determine for itself whether the electors designated in the certificate were properly chosen? Could it go even further beyond the certificate and decide whether voters in a particular state had been intimidated and prevented from casting their vote as a result?

Answers to these questions would determine whether the Commission would enter upon a wide-open inquiry of the same sort that the returning boards in Florida and Louisiana had undertaken. The issue was critical to both sides. If the Commission could hear witnesses and examine documents in the way that the congressional committees had done earlier, the proceedings would be greatly lengthened, and the Democrats could concentrate on their charge that, particularly in Louisiana, the returning board had acted fraudulently. If, on the other hand, the Commission's authority to go behind the certificates was nonexistent, or very limited, the Republicans would benefit. Thus the entire complicated political and procedural history of the Hayes–Tilden election and ultimately its outcome, had finally been reduced to the resolution of one issue: what was the scope of the Commission's review? If broad—as the Democrats urged—Tilden had a good chance; if narrow—as the Republicans wanted—Hayes would likely prevail.

It was generally agreed by both parties that the Commission could do no more than Congress itself in joint session as far as counting the electoral vote. And, of course, at this time in history "states' rights" were regarded with greater sanctity than they would be at a later date.

One of the ironies was that the Democrats were thought to be the party upholding states' rights, while the Republicans were the party who favored greater national authority. But advocates for the two parties experienced no difficulty in nimbly switching sides on this issue. The Republicans would suggest that for Congress or the Commission to "go behind the returns" was inconsistent with the division of authority between national and state governments which had been established by the Constitution. The Democrats would champion the authority of the national government to root out fraudulent returns by whatever means necessary. The Republicans conceded that while the certificates delivered to the President of the Senate were not "conclusive"— that is, immune from being attacked at all—they could be challenged only for forgery or for mistakes in naming the electors, and not by later executive or judicial action in the state which went beyond such challenge. The Democrats argued that fraud on the part of a returning board vitiated the entire state proceeding.

The question was exhaustively debated by extraordinarily able counsel on each side. Charles O'Conor, Jeremiah Black, and Richard Merrion spoke for the Democrats. Ashbel Green filed an impressive brief for them on the issue of whether the certificates were "conclusive." William M. Evarts, Matthew H. Carpenter, and Stanley Matthews—Hayes' college chum—spoke for the Republicans. On Monday, February 7, the Commission met at 11 a.m. to hear counsel argue the question of whether additional evidence, beyond the certificates, could be considered by the Commission. Bradley said he wished time to consider the matter, and Edmunds and Thurman concurred. The Commission thereupon adjourned until noon the following day.

When they reconvened, the members of the Commission stated their views on the issue of whether additional evidence should be considered. But most of them also discussed the related question of what effect the Florida court proceedings should have on the counting of that state's electoral vote. By the time each of them had spoken, the main issue in the Florida case was resolved on its merits. The congressional members of the Commission spoke first, and Garfield commented: "The proceedings were very impressive and the debate very able.... I have never spent a day in closer and severer intellectual work with more sharp incitement from the presence of able and trained minds."[3]

On the following day, the justices who were members of the Commission gave their opinions. Stephen Field's opinion, in support of receiving outside evidence, was representative of that of the other Democrats. He viewed the action of the Florida

Canvassing Board as simply "ministerial"—to declare who was elected as shown by the returns presented to them. In support of this position, he relied on the decision of the Supreme Court of Florida in *Drew v. Stearns,* which had faulted the canvassing board for throwing out some votes. And, said Field, when a state supreme court has spoken on the subject, that is considered to be state "law" just as surely as if it were embodied in a statute. Since the canvassing board had acted in excess of its authority, its action was invalid.

Field conceded that the Governor's certificate was "prima facie" evidence of the choice of electors, but concluded that countervailing evidence could be considered by the joint session of Congress, and therefore by the Commission. He pointed out that the decision of the trial court in the quo warranto case (a legal proceeding to determine who is entitled to a particular public office) was "the highest possible evidence of state action of the state of Florida, which although being appealed had the full force of law in the meantime." He also referred to the House committee which had investigated the returns and concluded that Tilden had received a majority of the votes in the state; the House had adopted a resolution to that effect by a party vote of 142 to 82.

Field's strongest point was probably the principle that a decision of a state's highest court was considered to be law just as surely as if enacted by the legislature. The Florida Supreme Court ruled that the State Canvassing Board acted improperly in disregarding returns which it believed to be fraudulent. He was on much weaker ground when he relied on a state trial court decision which was then being appealed, and on the findings of the House of Representatives based on its committee report, when the Senate—controlled by the Republicans—had reached a diametrically opposite result. He was concerned that a decision be had by March 4, which was the date for inaugurating the President, but thought this could be done by recognizing as controlling the decisions of the Florida courts and the conclusion of the House committee.

Justice Strong, a Republican commissioner, summarized his views in these words:

> My conclusions, then, are that neither Congress nor this commission has authority under the Constitution to recanvass the vote of Florida for state electors; that the first determination of the State canvassing-board was conclusive until it was reversed by state authority; that while it remained unreversed it conferred upon the persons declared by it to have been chosen electors rightful authority to cast the vote of the State; and that the act that those electors were appointed to do having been done, it was not in the power even of the State afterward to undo the act and call in question the authority by which it was done.[4]

This is an admirably concise statement of the views espoused by those who supported the cause of the Hayes electors. The state may provide methods for contesting the election of presidential electors, but such proceedings must be concluded by the time that the Constitution requires the electors to cast their votes. Once the duly certified electors have done so, later state court proceedings are of no effect. And Congress may not on its own recanvass the Florida vote.

Justice Miller, with his eye ever on practical considerations, said:

> It is strongly urged upon us that a large pile of papers, a half-bushel perhaps in quantity, of the contents of which both this

Commission and the two Houses of Congress are profoundly ignorant, has become legitimate evidence and must necessarily be considered by us, because they are in a very general way referred to in the papers filed by certain members of the two houses as their objection . . . to the certificate of Governor Stearns that the electors who have since cast their votes for Hayes and Wheeler were the duly appointed electors for the state of Florida. . . . No statement of the character, or nature, or source of a single paper, out of perhaps one hundred, is made. No reference is made to anything by which these papers can be identified. . . . They may be *ex parte* affidavits taken in the morasses of Florida, the slums of New York, or the private office of retained counsel in this city. It would be very strange indeed if the act of Congress under which we sit, intended to furnish in this manner the materials on which our decisions must be founded.[5]

He disagreed with Justice Field as to the weight which should be attached to the Florida court proceedings. He pointed out that these proceedings had taken place after the electors had cast their votes, and that the decision of the trial court in the quo warranto proceeding had been appealed by the Hayes electors. He went on to observe that if a single judge of a trial court might review the actions of the State Canvassing Board and set it aside, presumably any one of the many New York State trial judges could do the same and thereby at least render uncertain the casting of New York's 35 electoral votes. He concluded by saying:

Much has been said of the danger of the device of returning boards, and it may be that they have exercised their power in a manner not always worthy of commendation. But I take the liberty of saying that such a power lodged in one or in both Houses of Congress would be a far more permanent menace to the liberty of the people, to the legitimate result of the popular vote, than any device for counting those votes which has yet been adopted by states.[6]

In short, Justice Miller was of the view that deference should be given to the state returning boards and to the constitutionally imposed deadlines for the electors to cast their votes.

The opinion which was most eagerly awaited, of course, was that of Justice Bradley—the "casting vote." Garfield says:

> Judge Bradley arose at 2:13 to read his opinion. All were intent, because B. held the casting vote. It was a curious study to watch the faces as he read. All were making a manifest effort to appear unconcerned. It was ten minutes before it became evident that he was against the authority to hear extrinsic evidence. His opinion was clear and strong. . . .[7]

Bradley began by observing that the Commission could have no greater power than the two houses in joint session would have—common ground among all members of the Commission. He then inquired as to just what power the two houses could have. He first observed that the President of the Senate, by himself, exercised a purely ministerial function, and had no authority to do other than have the votes announced. In so holding, he rejected the arguments of Hayes and others that the President of the Senate had the authority to decide whether or not a particular vote should be counted.

Bradley observed that up until the electors cast their votes on the day prescribed by the Constitution, the entire election proceeding is in the hands of the states. He pointed out that the provision for the election of senators and representatives, where the

Constitution provided that "each House shall be the judge of the elections, returns and qualifications of its own members," was different from the provision concerning the election of the President. Both the House and the Senate were thereby authorized to make detailed inquiry into the claims of contesting candidates in congressional elections. But the absence of a similar provision in connection with the counting of electoral votes for President strongly suggested that no similar authority existed with respect to those votes.

He then stated that the two houses of Congress could certainly inquire whether the certificate presented had actually been signed by the executive, or whether the certificate contained a clear mistake of fact. The certificate, Bradley said, was a document of high authority, but not conclusive as to such cases. But in the present case there was no claim that the certificate of the Governor had been forged, or that there was any mistake of fact in it, or that it was willfully false and fraudulent. If erroneous at all, its error stemmed from erroneous proceedings of the canvassing board. But the canvassing board had been authorized by Florida law to decide which returns to be counted and had some authority to disregard false or fraudulent returns. The state itself could provide for any sort of election contest challenging the returns of the board so long as it was concluded by the time that the electors were to cast their vote in December. Here, of course, the state proceedings had occurred after that date.

Bradley then said that the decision of the Florida Supreme Court had only held that the board had acted mistakenly, although he conceded that the language of its opinion, if not its holding, had said that the canvassing board acted beyond its authority. But, he concluded, neither the state courts nor the Florida legislature—which had also intervened in the matter after the electors had cast their votes—could retroactively change the designation of electors after they had cast their votes and the certificate had gone to the President of the Senate.

In passing, he noted his agreement with Justice Miller's warning that the recognition of a congressional authority to recanvass state votes for presidential electors would be far more dangerous than any failure to correct fraud in a single state such as Florida.

Justice Clifford, as president of the commission, spoke last. The principal point he made, in addition to those made by Justice Field, was that the amount of evidence that the Commission would have to consider, if it went that route, was not great. He said that the Tilden electors were relying on returns from four Florida counties which had been thrown out in whole or in part by the State Canvassing Board, and that these county returns were on file with the Florida secretary of state.

He also argued that, legally, "fraud vitiates everything." In other words, if the canvassing board had acted fraudulently, it was just as if it had not acted at all. He concluded by saying:

> Prompt investigation was made by the new board of State canvassers, and the legislature enacted the statute declaring that the Tilden electors were duly chosen and appointed the next day after the decree was entered in the *quo warranto* suit. Neither the public nor the citizens have any power to defeat the machinations of fraud, perjury, and forgery if the measures adopted for that purpose in this case are held to be ineffectual and insufficient.[8]

There was a separate issue in the Florida case because it was claimed that F. C. Humphreys, one of the Hayes electors, had been appointed United States shipping commissioner by the Circuit Court for the Northern District of Florida. The Constitution, Article II, Section 1, provided that no "person holding an Office of Trust or Profit under the United States, shall be appointed an elector." On September 24, 1876, Humphreys had sent his resignation to Circuit Judge Woods, who was then out of the state. On October 2, Woods replied, "Your resignation is accepted. The vacancy can only be filled by the Circuit Court, and until I can go to Pensacola to open the court for that purpose, the duties of the office will have to be discharged by the collector."[9] The Tilden electors claimed that Humphreys' resignation could only be accepted when the court was in open session, and therefore Humphreys had never been validly chosen as an elector. Though this issue involved only one vote, it should be remembered that Hayes needed every one of the disputed votes in order to win; if Tilden could win only one of them, he would be President.

Bradley, though agreeing with the Hayes electors on the principal point at issue in Florida, held that evidence of Humphreys' appointment and resignation should be considered by the Commission. On Thursday, February 8, these witnesses confirmed the facts described above, and counsel argued the point. Bradley concluded that Humphreys had resigned his office before the election, but even had he not, he was a de facto elector and his vote should be counted.

Garfield then moved that the Commission find that the Hayes electors had been lawfully chosen, and the motion carried by a vote of 8 to 7—all of the Republicans voting for it and all of the Democrats voting against it. Senator Edmunds and Justices Miller and Bradley were appointed to draft a report to that effect; it was duly prepared, signed by the eight Republican members of the Commission, and sent to the President of the Senate. Upon the reading of the report to the joint session, the Senate withdrew to its chambers and promptly voted to sustain the decision of the Commission by a margin of 44 to 24. The House, after considerable debate, voted 168 to 103 to reject the report of the Commission. Since only one of the two houses had voted to overturn its report, the decision of the Commission was upheld and Florida's four electoral votes were counted for Hayes.

The tallying of the electoral votes by the joint session of Congress now resumed. The certificates from Georgia, Illinois, Indiana, and Iowa were not controverted. But then came Louisiana. Here, as with Florida, there were multiple certificates, members' objections to certificates unfavorable to their party, and a reference to the Electoral Commission.

The situation in Louisiana was different from that in Florida in at least two respects. First, there had been no court decisions in that state which attempted to decide the outcome of the election. Second, the returning board in Louisiana had thrown out not just a few votes, as was done in Florida, but thousands. Again, the question of "going behind the returns" and taking evidence was raised. Democrats spoke of fraud; Republicans spoke of intimidation of black voters. But after debate in closed session, the Commission by the same vote of 8 to 7 decided that it could not go behind the certificates and that the Hayes certificate was valid.

The joint session reconvened to receive the Commission's report; as with Florida, the Senate accepted it, and the House, after much rhetorical denunciation of the Commission, rejected it. Under the Electoral Commission law, Louisiana's votes, like Florida's, would be counted for Hayes.

Serious objections remained to be considered against the certificates of Oregon and South Carolina; both were referred to the Commission. That body decided by the familiar 8-to-7 margin that the Hayes certificate from each should be received. The Senate accepted, and the House rejected, these reports. But, beginning with the House debate on the Oregon certificate, a minority of Democrats began to delay proceedings in that body by offering dilatory proposals. One group, about forty in number, were the ones most outraged by what they regarded as the fraud on the nation perpetrated by the Republicans in general and by the Commission majority in particular. A second subset, mostly southerners, were willing to see the electoral count completed but in the meantime wanted to threaten the Republicans in order to extract some concessions from them.

These filibusters thought they would have at least the tacit support of the Speaker of the House, Samuel Randall of Pennsylvania. In the immediately preceding Congress, he had successfully held the floor for three days in an effort to defeat enactment of the Force bill. But now, as Speaker, he refused to entertain their motions, saying:

> The Chair rules that when the Constitution of the United States directs anything to be done, or when the law under the Constitution of the United States enacted in obedience thereto directs any act by this House, it is not in order to make any motion to obstruct or impede the execution of that injunction of the Constitution and the laws.[10]

Beginning in the last week of February, Hayes' supporters began making overtures to the southerners. Charles Foster, the representative from Hayes' own district in Ohio, said in a speech on the floor of the House that if Hayes were elected, "the flag should wave over states, not provinces." On February 26, three meetings were held in Washington between representatives of Hayes—Stanley Matthews, John Sherman, James Garfield, and William Dennison—and representatives of the southerners—

Representative John Young Brown of Kentucky, Senator J. B. Gordon of Georgia, Representative W. M. Levy of Louisiana, and Henry Watterson representing South Carolina. Out of these meetings came the following letter:

GENTLEMEN:

Referring to the conversation had with you yesterday, in which Governor Hayes's policy as to the status of certain states was discussed, we desire to say that we can assure you in the strongest possible manner of our great desire to have him adopt such a policy as will give to the people of the states of South Carolina and Louisiana the right to control their own affairs in their own way, subject only to the Constitution of the United States and the laws made in pursuance thereof, and to say further, that from an acquaintance with and knowledge of Governor Hayes and his views, we have the most complete confidence that such will be the policy of his administration.

Respectfully,
Stanley Matthews,
Charles Foster.

The southerners now began to withdraw their objections to the completion of the electoral count. After a rather spurious controversy over the electoral vote of Vermont—at that time as rock-ribbed a Republican state as there was—the count continued on to Wisconsin, the last state in the alphabetical order. Democrats attacked one of its electors as a federal employee and therefore ineligible. The debate carried over into the early morning hours of March 2. At about 4 a.m., the count was complete, and the President of the Senate, before declaring Hayes elected, commented:

> In announcing the final result of the electoral vote the Chair trusts that all present, whether on the floor or in the galleries, will refrain from all demonstration whatever; that nothing shall transpire on this occasion to mar the dignity and moderation which have characterized these proceedings, in the main so reputable to the American people and worthy of the respect of the world.[11]

— CHAPTER 9 —

THE ELECTORAL COMMISSION'S DECISIONS were roundly
denounced by the Democrats and heartily praised by the
Republicans. Although eight members of the Commission had
voted to sustain Hayes' claims to the presidency, Bradley alone
was singled out for special opprobrium. There were two reasons
for this: First, because he was the "casting vote" among the fifteen members, replacing David Davis, who was thought to be a
genuine Independent. Second, because he was believed to have
changed his vote at the last minute at the behest of Republican
friends.

Bradley was indeed the "casting vote" on a commission composed of seven Democrats, seven Republicans, and himself. But
his selection in that capacity cannot have been welcome to him.
He was identified with the Republican Party. If in good con-
science he concluded that its arguments should prevail, he would
nonetheless be denounced as a partisan, in a way that Davis
would not have been had his reasoning followed the same course.

The arguments in favor of Tilden were easier to grasp than
those in favor of Hayes. Tilden had won a majority of the popular vote, and there was strong evidence that at least in Louisiana

a partisan returning board had fraudulently disallowed more than enough returns to deny him the state's electoral votes. The charge against the board was not simply incompetence, or negligence, but fraud—deliberate tampering with the returns to pro-

"The Electorial Committee in session in the Supreme Court Chamber,"
from the February 17, 1877, issue of Harper's Weekly.

duce the outcome desired by the board. The fact that all four members of the board were Republicans, and that its chairman, Madison Wells, had an unsavory reputation, lent substance to the charge. Surely there must be some way to remedy this wrong and award the presidency to Tilden, who had rightly earned it.

The reasoning of the pro-Hayes Republicans was far more complicated and must be placed in the context of the times to be fully understood. The Englishman James Bryce wrote a well-regarded study of the American system of government entitled *The American Commonwealth* in 1889. He relates the following incident:

> Some years ago the American Protestant Episcopal Church was occupied at its triennial Convention in revising its liturgy. It was thought desirable to introduce among the short sentence prayers a prayer for the whole people; and an eminent New England divine proposed the words "Oh Lord, bless our nation." Accepted one afternoon on the spur of the moment, the sentence was brought up next day for reconsideration, when so many objections were raised by the laity to the word "nation," as importing too definite a recognition of national unity, that it was dropped, and instead there were adopted the words "Oh Lord, bless these United States."[1]

There was not only a different perception of the relationship between the states and the nation at this time than there is today, but the reality was, in fact, quite different. Until the Civil War, Congress had followed what might be called the "night watchman" principle of government. It provided for the common defense, delivered the mail, collected customs duties at the country's ports, and left the remainder of governing to the states. All of this was beginning to change with the industrialization following the Civil War, but in 1876 most of the change toward a more active federal government lay in the future.

Structurally, too, the system of national government gave the states a greater role than it does now. Today, members of the United States Senate are elected by popular vote in their respective states. But it took the Seventeenth Amendment to the Constitution, adopted in 1913, to bring that about. Before then, the legislatures of each state elected its senators. When, after the Lincoln-Douglas debates in 1858, Illinois picked Stephen A. Douglas as its senator, the choice was made not by popular vote but by the Illinois legislature. State legislatures did not hesitate to attempt to instruct the senators they had chosen as to how to vote on a matter pending in the Senate. Senators were thought of as representing their states as entities, as well as the people in their states, to a degree that lessened with the Seventeenth Amendment.

In the Hayes–Tilden dispute, this concept of state sovereignty played an important role. Everyone agreed that the Electoral Commission could do no more by way of investigation of state election returns than Congress itself could do. The Republican position was that the Constitution left the choice of electors to the states, and that with rare exceptions Congress could not "go behind" the certificates which they sent to the President of the Senate. It could not, therefore, examine the correctness of the vote count certified by state officials. While a state itself could provide for challenges to the count, those challenges had to be concluded by the December date on which the electors meet and cast their votes. Once the designated electors had done this, no later state proceedings (such as those in Florida) could occur, and Congress itself could not conduct a reexamination of the outcome of the election.

The Republican position was based not only on the Constitution but also on fear for the consequences if congressional reexamination were allowed. The question to be examined, of course, was which candidate had actually received the majority of votes cast in a given state. But how would the Commission (or in future cases, the joint session of Congress) go about this? Justice Field suggested that they need only consult the majority report of the committee of the House of Representatives which had toured the disputed states after the election and concluded that Tilden had won Florida and Louisiana. But this was hardly acceptable to the Republicans. The House was controlled by Democrats, and the Republican-controlled Senate majority report had come to the exact opposite conclusion.

David Dudley Field told the Commission that he was prepared to prove by "clouds of witnesses and by a host of documents" that Tilden had carried Florida. Justice Miller described the material offered to the Commission as "a large pile of papers, a half-bushel perhaps in quantity. . . . They may be *ex parte* affidavits taken in the morasses of Florida, the slums of New York, the private office of retained counsel in this city."

The returning boards themselves merely received tallies compiled by voting officials in the various counties or parishes of the state in question. If the Commission could review the conclusions of these state returning boards, could it also examine the tallies compiled in each county? What would be the basis of the challenges? The Democrats emphasized the likelihood of fraud—that returning boards had disallowed proper votes in order to reach a desired result. The Republicans spoke of intimidation of black voters—would this, too, be a permissible issue? If so, there was an added difficulty in that the chain of causation was much more indirect and difficult to prove. If night riders had gone through a town two weeks before the election, would claims be entertained that black voters refrained from voting because of this?

Since the Electoral Commission refused to receive any of the evidence offered, it is not possible to say how time-consuming even an inquiry into the claims of fraud would have been, or how clear-cut any result would have been. Perhaps a truly independent commission could, in due time, have produced satisfactory proof that, at least in Louisiana, Tilden had received a majority of the vote. But at what cost in terms of future challenges in close presidential elections? If control of the House and Senate in future contests were divided between the two parties, as it was in 1876, the result would likely have been the creation of another electoral commission, with the same number of partisans on each side, and one presumed neutral member who would in fact decide the issue for the entire commission.

But if both houses were controlled by the same party, there would be no need for a commission. Congress could appoint a joint committee to examine and report, with some suspicion that the result was foreordained. Each House of Congress would go through this process in connection with challenges to the election of its own members, but the Constitution expressly confers this authority upon it. There is no similar constitutional provision in the case of counting the electoral votes for President.

One need not choose between the Democratic and Republican arguments to say that the position accepted by Bradley was a reasonable one. Two contemporaneous sources confirm at least the reasonableness, if not the outright correctness, of Bradley's stance. First is the comment of David Davis himself on the matter, Davis having been viewed as a true Independent by members of both parties. Privately he said of Bradley's position, "No good lawyer, not a strict partisan, could decide otherwise."[2]

The second support for Bradley's position came in an earlier Senate debate predating the Hayes–Tilden contest when there was no actual dispute over the counting of electoral votes and neither party had an ax to grind. Congress, in February 1865, had adopted Joint Rule 22, which provided that, when electoral votes were being counted in the joint session of Congress, "no vote objected to shall be counted except by the concurring vote of the two Houses." In 1875, the Senate debated a proposal by Senator Morton of Indiana to amend Joint Rule 22 and provide that "no objection to any such vote shall be valid unless such objection is sustained by an affirmative vote by both Houses." The effect of this proposal would be to reverse the principle of Rule 22—instead of requiring both houses' concurrence to *overrule* an objection, it would require such a vote to *sustain* an objection. That is to say, no objection could prevent an electoral vote from being counted unless both houses of Congress agreed.

In the ensuing debate, some of the Senate's ablest members expressed their views on the general subject. No measure was actually adopted, but there was substantive agreement on both sides of the aisle that in its consideration of an objection Congress could not "go behind" the certifications sent in by the states. Professor Charles Fairman states that this was "the view of Thurman, Bayard, and other Democrats, as well as of Frelinghuysen and other Republicans in the debates of 1875 and 1876: 'It *could not be done.*' "[3]

IT WAS MORE COMMON IN 1876 than now for newspapers to be openly aligned with one political party. The *New York Times,* for example, was identified with the Republican Party and, as noted in Chapter 5, reported the election result in such a way as to offer a scenario for a Hayes victory. Two other New York papers—the *World* and the *Sun*—were identified with the Democratic Party. The *Sun* conducted what might be called a vendetta against Bradley.

On February 11, after the Florida case had been decided by the Electoral Commission, the *Sun* opined that there was "no process or method by which fraud can be converted into honest reality . . . [but] Judge Bradley seems today to have the ability, as well as the intention, to attempt such a miracle."[4]

The *Sun* returned to the fray during the summer, saying,

"The two blackened Judges [Strong and Bradley] were members of the Electoral Commission, and they delivered over the Presidency, just as they had foresworn themselves in the legal tender case, being operated upon by the same corrupt influences in both instances. Bradley, especially, will be known in history as the infamous eighth man who, without scruple and without shame, cast his vote every time to uphold the frauds of the Returning Boards, and violently contradicted his own positions to maintain the corrupt conspiracy."[5]

But then a month later, the *Sun* took a new tack, charging that Bradley had changed his vote on the Commission at the behest of midnight callers the previous evening.

AN INTERESTING HISTORICAL FACT:

After the argument on the Florida case . . . Justice Bradley wrote out his opinion and his decision in full. He completed it at about 6 o'clock in the evening on the day before the judgment of the Commission was to be announced, and read it to Judge Clifford and Judge Field. . . . It contained first, an argument, and secondly, a conclusion. The argument was precisely the same as that which appears in the published document, but Judge Bradley's conclusion was that the votes of the Tilden electors in Florida were the only votes that ought to be counted as coming from that State.

This was the character of the paper when Judge Bradley finished it, and when he communicated it to his colleagues. During the whole of that night Judge Bradley's house in Washington was surrounded by carriages of visitors who came to see him. . . .

When the Commission assembled the next morning and when the judgment was declared, Judge Bradley gave his vote in favor of counting the votes of the Hayes electors in

Florida! The argument he did not deliver at the time, but when it came to be printed subsequently it was found to be precisely the same as the argument which he had originally drawn up and on which he had based his first conclusion in favor of the Tilden electors.[6]

As Professor Fairman points out, no authority was cited for any of these facts. The Commission itself was sitting at 6 p.m. on the day before its decision was released and did not adjourn until 7:45 p.m. This was the day on which nine of the ten congressional members of the Commission gave their opinions and votes. An argument that supported the Tilden position until it came to the sort of O. Henry ending envisioned by the *Sun* article is contradicted by Garfield's contemporary entry:

It was ten minutes before it became evident that he was against the authority to hear extrinsic evidence. His opinion was clear and strong. Near the close he surprised us all by holding that we could hear testimony on the eligibility of Humphreys.[7]

The "surprise" referenced by Garfield was *not* Bradley's conclusion that the Commission could not consider outside evidence. The surprise was Bradley's agreement with the Democrats to hear evidence on the eligibility of Humphreys, one of the Florida Republican electors. This, however, was the very sort of issue that Bradley thought was proper for the Commission to consider and is entirely consistent with the conclusion that the Commission could not "go behind" the certificates and attempt a recanvass of the votes cast.

Justice Field, as might be expected, was bitterly disappointed that the Commission had decided the case against Tilden. On April 2, he wrote to Matthew Deady, the federal district judge in Oregon, whom he saw while sitting on circuit on the West Coast:

> The decision of the Commission, not to enquire into the correctness of the action of the Canvassing Boards of Louisiana and Florida was a great shock to the country. It is the first time, I believe, that it has ever been held by any respectable body of jurists, that a fraud was protected from exposure by a certificate by its authors. I shall have much to say to you during the summer of the proceedings before that Tribunal and of its action. The President, who owes his seat to the success of a gigantic conspiracy and fraud, is not finding his place a bed of roses. It is right that it should be so. He is evidently a very weak man, and hardly knows what to do. . . . [8]

When Field was questioned by reporters in California about the story in the *Sun,* reporting that Bradley had read an opinion to him and Clifford, the *Newark Daily Advertiser* reported:

> The Daily Exchange to-day publishes an interview with Justice Field. According to the statement of the reporter he had first objected to giving any statement whatever, but finally said after some reflection, and speaking with great deliberation, "Well, sir, all that I care to say . . . is that Justice Bradley read (with peculiar emphasis on the word read) no opinion to me in advance of the formal submission of the opinions to the Commission."[9]

Finally, on September 3, the *Newark Daily Advertiser* published a letter from Bradley himself:

Stowe, Vt., Sept. 2, 1877
EDITOR OF THE Advertiser:

—I perceive that the New York *Sun* has reiterated its
charge that after preparing a written opinion in favor of the
Tilden electors in the Florida case, submitted to the Electoral Commission, I changed my views during the night
preceding the vote, in consequence of pressure brought to
bear upon me by Republican politicians and Pacific Railroad men, whose carriages, it is said, surrounded my house
during the evening. This, I believe, is the important point of
the charge. Whether I wrote one opinion, or twenty, in my
private examination of the subject, is of little consequence,
and of no concern to anybody, if the opinion which I finally
gave was the fair result of my deliberations, without influence from outside parties. The above slander was published
some time since, but I never saw it until recently, and
deemed it too absurd to need refutation. But as it is categor-
ically repeated, perhaps I ought to notice it. The same story
about carriages of leading Republicans, and others, congre-
gating at my house, was circulated at Washington at the
same time, and came to the ears of my family, only to raise a
smile of contempt. The whole thing is a falsehood. Not a
single visitor called at my house that evening; and during
the whole sitting of the Commission, I had no private discussion whatever on the subjects at issue with any person
interested on the Republican side, and but very few words
with any person. Indeed, I sedulously sought to avoid all
discussion outside the Commission itself. The allegation
that I read an opinion to Judges Clifford and Field is
entirely untrue. I read no opinion to either of them, and
have no recollection of expressing any. If I did, it could only

have been suggestively, or in a hypothetical manner, and not intended as a committal of my final judgement or action. The question was one of grave importance, and, to me, of much difficulty and embarrassment. I earnestly endeavored to come to a right decision, free from all political or other extraneous considerations. In my private examination of the principal question (about going behind the returns), I wrote and re-wrote the arguments and considerations on both sides as they occurred to me, sometimes being inclined to one view of the subject, and sometimes to the other. But finally I threw aside these lucubrations, and, as you have rightly stated, wrote out the short opinion which I read in the Florida case during the sitting of the Commission. This opinion expresses the honest conclusion to which I had arrived, and which, after a full consideration of the whole matter, seemed to me the only satisfactory solution of the question. And I may add, that the more I have reflected on it since, the more satisfied have I become that it was right. At all events, it was the result of my own reflections and consideration, without any suggestion from any quarter, except the arguments adduced by counsel in the public discussion, and by the members of the Commission in its private consultations.[10]

Thus matters stood for nearly three-quarters of a century, until historian Allan Nevins' biography of Abram Hewitt was published in 1935.[11] Hewitt, it will be recalled, was the chairman of the Democratic National Committee during the election of 1876 and its aftermath.

In the early 1870s, Hewitt became active in the byzantine politics of New York City. He joined in the efforts to reform Tammany Hall and topple Boss Tweed. He lived in New York City, near Tilden. The two had known each other for some time, and became close friends. Tilden handpicked one of the congressional districts in Manhattan for which Hewitt would successfully run as a Democratic candidate in 1874.

Justice Samuel Miller, 1876.

Hewitt played no contemporary part in the attack on Bradley, but he had compiled what he called a "Secret History" of the disputed election, an account which lay dormant long after he died in 1903. But Nevins' biography drew heavily on it, in particular in its account of Bradley's decision as a member of the Electoral Commission. The only account of its origin given by Nevins is this:

> Two years later he wrote out a secret history of the disputed election, which in 1895 he re-wrote and amplified. In this history, which he directed should never be published until all the men named therein were dead, he gave his own story of a contest in which, both as congressional leader and Democratic National Chairman, he played a vital role.[12]

Hewitt gives this account of Bradley's vote on the Electoral Commission in the "Secret History":

> The history of this opinion forms an important feature in the final outcome of the electoral count. As stated above, Mr. John G. Stevens was the intimate friend of Judge Bradley. He passed the night previous to the rendition of the judgment in the Florida case at my house. About midnight he returned from a visit to Judge Bradley, and reported to General Richard Taylor, who was also staying with me, and to Senator Gibson, who was awaiting his return, that he had just left Judge Bradley after reading his opinion in favor of counting the vote of the Democratic electors of the State of Florida. Such a judgment insured the election of Tilden to the Presidency with three votes to spare above the necessary majority. We parted, therefore, with the assurance that all further doubt as to the Presidency was at rest. I attended the delivery of the judgment the next day without the slightest intimation from any quarter that Judge Bradley had changed

his mind. In fact, the reading of the opinion until the few concluding paragraphs were reached was strictly in accordance with the report of Mr. Stevens.

The change was made between midnight and sunrise. Mr. Stevens afterwards informed me that it was due to a visit to Judge Bradley by Senator Frelinghuysen and Secretary Robeson, made after his departure. Their appeals to Judge Bradley were said to have been reinforced by the persuasion of Mrs. Bradley. Whatever the fact may have been, Judge Bradley himself in a subsequent letter addressed to the *Newark Daily Advertiser* admitted that he had written a favorable opinion which on subsequent reflection he saw fit to modify.

What to make of this? Even the sketchy description of the origin of the "Secret History" raises warning signals for anyone writing a history. There is no indication that the account was based on Hewitt's contemporary notes; it appears that it was first written down from memory two years after the event—in 1879, that is—and then "revised and amplified" sixteen years later, in 1895. In 1879, two years after the events recounted, Hewitt was fifty-seven years old; in 1895, he was seventy-three years old. The portion of the account written in 1879 could be expected to have some mistakes in it, but that so much of it was "amplified" in 1895 made it dubious indeed.

From the part of the "history" quoted by Nevins, it is difficult to tell which is which. But even from the quoted sections, there is evidence that they themselves were the subject of the 1895 "amplification." Hewitt first turns his attention to Bradley before the latter was chosen for the Commission. Speaking of the Democratic position after Davis had withdrawn his name from consideration for the Electoral Commission, he says:

Practically, therefore, the choice was limited to Justice Bradley, whom I had personally known for many years in New Jersey as a very able lawyer and a man of the highest integrity. The confidence which I felt in him was shared by Mr. Tilden, but in order to make assurance doubly sure I requested a mutual friend of Judge Bradley and myself, the late John G. Stevens of Trenton, New Jersey, to confer with Judge Bradley to ascertain whether he felt that he could decide the questions which would come before the Commission without prejudice or party feeling. The report of Mr. Stevens was entirely satisfactory.[13]

Two facts in connection with this one paragraph are worth noting. First, Bradley was regarded as a person of the highest integrity. Second, and perhaps more important, the paragraph refers to the *late* John G. Stevens. But Stevens did not die until 1886, when he committed suicide. (He had been subject to fits of depression.) Thus it is probable that the paragraph was at least amplified, if not composed, in 1895.

When we look at the full statement of Bradley's supposed activities quoted on pages 193–194, it is at least in one important respect inconsistent with known facts. There is no way in which Hewitt could have "attended the delivery of the judgment the next day" and heard Bradley read his opinion. The opinions were read in a secret session of the Electoral Commission. The public was not informed of the Commission's decision not to receive extrinsic evidence until late in the afternoon, after Miller's motion had been carried in the closed session. The actual written opinions of the members were not made public until late February.

Garfield's diary entry, as well as Bradley's opinion itself, contradicts that part of the account which says that until the concluding paragraphs it appeared that Bradley would rule for Tilden. Bradley's opinion is entirely consistent and quite organized; there was a surprise at the end, but that was with respect to taking extrinsic evidence on the claim against Humphreys as an elector.

In a court of law, one may testify to facts which he knows of his own knowledge, but not to those which he learns from others (the hearsay rule). Thus, for example, if Stevens came to Hewitt and told him that Bradley has said he will vote for Tilden, Hewitt may not testify to that fact although Stevens may. History would be undoubtedly the poorer and sparser if the hearsay rule were applied to the reconstruction of events such as the disputed election of 1876, but certainly firsthand knowledge is to be preferred over second- and thirdhand.

With respect to the opinion which Stevens says Bradley showed him, we must consider Stevens' credibility as well as Hewitt's. It seems odd that even a good friend would have called on Bradley so late in the evening and then be shown an opinion which would be read in a closed session the following day. It also seems odd that Bradley—a member of the Supreme Court for eight years, where absolute secrecy about opinions is customary until they are released to the public—would have shown his opinion to Stevens. These objections, of course, cannot prove that Stevens' account was false, but they do raise questions about it.

Stevens was a wealthy New Jersey industrialist who committed suicide in 1886. The *New York Times* said in the final paragraph of his obituary:

> ... Mr. Stevens's family has been one of great prominence, socially and financially. He, however, has of recent years been reported to be in embarrassed circumstances. Something over a year ago he was found nearly suffocated with

gas in a room in Sixth-avenue, New York. Once before, it is said, he took an overdose of chloral and nearly died. Two of his brothers are said to have been inmates of insane asylums.

If Stevens himself had recorded the account of his visit to Bradley's home, his credibility would have to be tested against Bradley's, who flatly denied that anyone had visited him. But Stevens recorded nothing; what has survived is Hewitt's account of what Stevens told him.

When we look at the next part of the account—the supposed change in the opinion "between midnight and sunrise" at the behest of Senator Frelinghuysen and Naval Secretary George Robeson—the credibility becomes much more strained. Hewitt says that Stevens "afterwards" informed him of this fact. When? A day later? Two years later? And how did Stevens know? The claimed visit of Frelinghuysen and Robeson by Stevens' own account took place after he left Bradley's house near midnight. So he could not have been present when the midnight visitors arrived. What is the basis for his knowledge of the visit? We are left to guess. And how likely is it that Frelinghuysen and Robeson—admittedly friends of Bradley's—would have visited him after midnight to find out how he was going to vote? Frelinghuysen was a member of the Commission as well as a friend, and would have had ample opportunity at previous sessions of that body to make inquiry if he chose to do so.

Finally, why compile a "Secret History" of a very important event, with instructions that it be released only after the death of everyone who had participated? Members of the Supreme Court have had to confront a similar situation in dealing with their records of their deliberations in conference. Conferences are closed to the public, and records of these deliberations are regarded as absolutely privileged and confidential, in order to assure that each member of the conference will speak with complete candor on the issues of each case. But it is generally agreed that history also has its claims, and that eventually these records should be available to the public. An embargo of the sort which Hewitt put on his "Secret History" would make sense for the records of the Court's conference. But there seems to be no reason to think that any similar concerns attended Hewitt's memoir—there is no indication of any pledge of secrecy to the people who had given him information. Had Hewitt's "Secret History" been made public when it was first composed in 1879, the various participants would have had an opportunity to comment on it, and Hewitt would not have had an opportunity to revise it sixteen years later.

Nevins gives his own evaluation of Hewitt's "Secret History":

This statement in all probability explains Bradley's mysterious vote. Rumors of what had happened that fateful night were soon bruited abroad, some very inaccurate and unfair. Judge Bradley later seized upon these reports, one of which included the harsh accusation that he had succumbed to pressure from Texas Pacific Railroad magnates, to issue a long statement. He admitted that he had written a decision favorable to Tilden. But he explained that he had followed the alleged practice of some jurists in writing out two opinions, thus giving the arguments on both sides, and intending to accept in the end whichever seemed the stronger. In a world where anything is possible, this is possible. But it is certainly hard to believe. If the practice mentioned ever existed, it was excessively rare. There was no need to write out the argument, for they lay in printed form before the judges. Bradley's quick, clear mind was one of the last on the tribunal to require such aid. Moreover, the vital question of

going behind the returns was not complex and did not
require elaborate argument—it was a very simple issue of
principle.[14]

To say that there was no need to write out the arguments
because they were contained in briefs is to take some liberty with
the facts and to fail to understand the preparation of judicial
opinions on different questions. What Bradley actually said was
that he "wrote and re-wrote the arguments and considerations
on both sides." Surely this does not mean that he mechanically
copied first from one brief and then from the other. First and
foremost, most of the arguments of counsel had been oral. There
were only three written briefs submitted, and all of those were
on behalf of Tilden: no written briefs were submitted on behalf
of Hayes. Second, a judge must know, and understand to the
best of his ability, the arguments made by each party. In a case
which is squarely controlled by previous decisions this may be
enough. But in a difficult case raising novel questions, it is not.
Briefs, even good briefs, may be like two ships passing in the
night, neither one squarely dealing with the arguments of the
other. The all-important process of bringing to bear one's judgment is a good deal more than reciting the arguments on each
side and announcing the results.

To say that the "vital question of going behind the returns
was not complex and did not require elaborate argument—it
was a very simple issue of principle" is not only to subscribe to
the arguments of the Tilden supporters, but to declare that there
is nothing to be said on the other side. Surely the arguments pro
and con set forth at the beginning of this chapter dispose of this
simplistic proposition. There was more than one "principle"
involved, as there is in most important cases.

Nevins' treatment of this subject is, I believe, flawed in two respects. First, he gives uncritical credence to Hewitt's "Secret History," and then compounds this mistake by giving his own one-sided assessment of the merits of the case before the Electoral Commission.

When Hewitt appraised Bradley as a possible member of the Commission, he considered him as "a very able lawyer and man of the highest integrity." Surely that reputation should have weight in deciding between the unsupported accounts in the *New York Sun* and Hewitt's "Secret History" on the one hand, and Bradley's flat denial of the principal thrust of those accounts on the other. No one writing at the present time can know for certain where the truth lies, but, it would seem, the very most those accounts warrant is a Scottish verdict of "not proven."

— CHAPTER 10 —

HAYES AND HIS FAMILY remained in Columbus until the counting of the electoral vote by Congress was nearly finished. They then boarded a train for Washington, and near Harrisburg the President-elect received word that Senate President Ferry had declared him elected President, and Congress had adjourned. Because March 4 fell on a Sunday, the formal inauguration ceremony was scheduled for Monday. But to avoid any possible disruption, the new President was privately sworn in at the White House on Sunday, March 4. Both Stephen Field and Nathan Clifford boycotted the public ceremony on Monday; indeed, Clifford would never set foot in the White House during Hayes' term as President.

The newly elected leader faced a difficult task. Half of the nation regarded his presidency as illegitimate, and his opponents referred to him as "Rutherfraud." His own party preferred him to Tilden, but was by no means united on the questions with which he would have to deal. Elements in the party wanted civil service reform, but the Senate's Republican barons were determined to retain their patronage prerogatives. He would confront the necessity of pulling the last federal troops out of the former

Confederacy, the question of civil service reform, the "currency questions": still in a depression, renewed demands for inflationary measures came from farmers and from the western states.

Hayes appointed a strong cabinet, headed by William Maxwell Evarts as Secretary of State, John Sherman as Secretary of the Treasury, and Carl Schurz as Secretary of the Interior. Evarts was a highly respected New York lawyer who had overseen much of the advocacy on Hayes' behalf before the Electoral Commission. Sherman, a fellow Ohioan, was knowledgeable

William Evarts, c. 1860s–1870s.

about finances from his service in the Senate. Schurz was a long-time champion of civil service reform and therefore obnoxious to the Senate barons. Hayes failed to consult with any of the party leaders about his cabinet, and the Senate took revenge by referring all of the nominations to committees—even that of its own member John Sherman. Though each nominee was in due course confirmed, the Senate's initial rebuff to Hayes was a harbinger of strained relations over patronage matters.

Hayes had never explicitly approved the commitment made by his lieutenants to remove federal troops from Louisiana and Florida. Grant had begun the process just before he left office but postponed further actions at Hayes' request. The new President wished to extract, from the Democratic governors who would come into power upon the removal of the troops, a commitment that they would respect the rights of blacks under the Civil War Amendments to the Constitution. The governors duly promised, and the troops were removed shortly after Hayes took office. But the promises were honored largely in the breach.

Hayes had little choice in the matter. Democrats in the House had already refused to appropriate funds for the continued use of troops. Northern public opinion had over time swung against the use of soldiers for this purpose in the South. Hayes has been criticized for ordering the withdrawal, but he had no practicable alternative. Surely if Tilden had been elected he would have done exactly the same thing.

Hayes championed civil service reform to a greater extent than any of his predecessors. In June 1877, he ordered federal officeholders not to participate in elective politics, and prohibited the traditional assessments of federal employees to finance the campaigns of the party in power. These orders were by no means instantly heeded across the board, and they antagonized powerful senators—none more than New York's Roscoe Conkling.

The biggest New York patronage plum was the office of collector of the Port of New York: the collector supervised the collection of tariffs at the nation's busiest port, and was rewarded with a large income in doing so.

Following the report of a commission that the dubious practices of the current collector, Chester A. Arthur, had cost the government up to one-quarter of its lawful revenues, Hayes in September 1877 announced that Arthur and his second-in-command, Alonzo Cornell, would be removed from office. Conkling struck back a few days later at the New York State Republican Convention, where his handpicked delegates adopted a platform that completely ignored the administration in Washington. Hayes nominated two members of the Reform wing of the New York party to succeed Arthur and Cornell. In November, the Senate Commerce Committee, chaired by Conkling, voted to reject the nominees. Behind this action was the doctrine of senatorial control of patronage in their respective states. The battle between the President and Conkling waged over a period of several years, but Hayes' persistence won out, and his nominees to the New York Customs House were confirmed over Conkling's violent opposition.

IN JULY 1877, a major railroad strike occurred, affecting all of the roads moving goods between the Northeast and the Midwest. The effects of the depression still remained, and the railroads were competing with one another for a shrinking volume of freight. They therefore reduced their rates for carriage and sought to balance this loss of revenue by cutting the wages of workers. In June the Pennsylvania Railroad announced that it would cut wages by 10 percent, and shortly afterward the Baltimore & Ohio, the Erie, and the New York Central Railroads followed suit. In mid-July, employees struck at the principal points along the Baltimore & Ohio Railroad. Police in Baltimore suppressed the strikers there, but in Martinsburg, West Virginia, the workers and their allies halted freight trains, backing up traffic on the road's main line to the West.

John W. Garrett, president of the B&O, asked Governor Henry M. Mathews of West Virginia to request federal troops. Matthews made the appeal to Hayes, asking for 200 to 300 troops to restore order in Martinsburg. The request was sketchy as to the situation there, and Hayes asked for further information. The Governor responded that without such assistance much property would be destroyed. Hayes then ordered federal troops from the Washington arsenal and Fort McHenry in Baltimore to Martinsburg. By the time they arrived, the city was calm, but on the next day rioting broke out in Baltimore. Militia troops were stoned, and responded by opening fire on the strikers, killing several of them. A mob then burned nearby railroad passenger cars and part of the depot. Maryland Governor John Lee Carroll requested federal troops and received them.

Now the rioting spread to Pittsburgh, where neither the local police nor local elements of the state National Guard restored order along the line of the Pennsylvania Railroad. National Guard troops sent from Philadelphia succeeded briefly in doing this, but they were then besieged in a roundhouse and forced to evacuate. Thomas Scott, the president of the Pennsylvania Railroad, Governor Hartranft, and Pittsburgh Mayor William Stokeley, requested Hayes to send troops not merely to keep the peace, but to put down the strike.

At this time, of course, there were no federal labor laws, scarcely any precedents for presidential action in such a situation. Upon receiving this request, Hayes convened his cabinet at 10 p.m. on a Sunday evening. The administration was gradually developing a policy governing responses to calls for federal troops. Soldiers were dispatched even without a request to protect United States property, such as arsenals. But a formal appeal for assistance was required in other cases, and the military was only made available subject to the direction of local authorities. Scott's request for federal troops to operate trains carrying United States mail was refused, because the strikers shrewdly let mail trains go through.

The strike spread further, to Buffalo and St. Louis. Most of the press sided with management, raising the specter of the Paris Commune a few years before. But Hayes refused to be panicked, and the strike was over by the end of July. The President was willing to see the two sides fight the matter out with economic weapons, even at the cost of serious interruption of rail traffic— so long as law and order prevailed and government property was secure.

THE PREVIOUSLY ENACTED Resumption Act called for redemption of greenbacks with gold beginning in 1879. But desire for debtor relief in some form was spreading from farmers and westerners to the Midwest as well. During a special session of Congress in late 1877, the House passed the Bland Act, calling for unlimited coinage of silver at the rate of 16 to 1 for gold. Hayes had an almost religious trust in the gold standard, and strongly opposed the Bland bill. But Senator William Allison of Iowa proposed in the Senate that the coinage of silver be allowed, but instead of being unlimited, the government should be required to coin 2 to 4 million silver dollars every month. This provision placed a limit on silver coinage and left substantial discretion to the government below that limit. While supporters of unlimited coinage of silver did not have the votes to override a veto by

Hayes, both houses enacted the Bland–Allison Act, which called for limited coinage of silver, and overrode Hayes' veto. This battle would be fought again in the 1896 presidential campaign between William McKinley and William Jennings Bryan.

In the spring of 1878, the Democratic majority in the House created a special committee—called the "Potter Committee" after its chairman, Representative Clarkson Potter of New York—to investigate alleged fraud in the 1876 presidential elections in Florida and Louisiana. The committee heard testimony that several election officials in those states had been offered federal jobs if they would "keep the faith," but most of the testimony was secondhand. The Republican minority of the committee brought to light a bribery offer by Tilden's nephew but never traced it back to the candidate himself. The efforts of the committee led to no legislation or other action.

IN THE OFF-YEAR ELECTION of 1878, the Democrats not only retained control of the House of Representatives, but gained a majority of the Senate as well. Hayes would now face a Congress entirely controlled by the opposition party. One of the objects of this new Congress was to repeal the Force Act, enacted during the Grant administration. It provided for various forms of federal supervision over elections for federal officeholders. Over a period of many months, Congress sought to accomplish its repeal in two different ways: first, by attaching a "rider" to a bill whose main purpose was to appropriate money for the operation of the federal government; second, by enacting the repealer as a separate, substantive bill. Appropriations bill riders are a form of political hardball, not to say blackmail. Knowing that the President must have funds appropriated to run the government, Congress says, "Here are the funds you need, but you may have them only on the condition that you accept the rider as well, a provision we know you would veto if it were passed as a separate bill." Hayes vetoed no less than four of these efforts, and in each case the House of Representatives was unable to muster the necessary two-thirds majority to override him.

AT THE BEGINNING of his term as President, Hayes declared that he would not be a candidate for reelection. Although urged from time to time to repudiate his declaration, he stuck with it. He remained neutral during the contest for the Republican nomination in 1880, when James A. Garfield won the nomination on the thirty-fifth ballot.

Various rankings of presidents generally show Hayes as "average," and there seems little reason to quarrel with this assessment. The presidents rated as "great"—Abraham Lincoln, George Washington, and Franklin D. Roosevelt—held the office at a time in which events critical to the nation's destiny were occurring. For Lincoln it was the Civil War, for Washington it was the formative stage of the new government, for Roosevelt it was World War II. Hayes presided during a much less turbulent era, and it is doubtful that Lincoln, Washington, or Roosevelt would have been called "great" had they held office at that time.

Tilden's biographer Alexander Clarence Flick, writing in 1939, observed that, "although confronted by hostile Democrats who controlled the House for four years and the Senate too, and by an unsympathetic group of Republicans, [the Hayes] administration was enlightened and able."[1] The Hayes era, of course, differed greatly from the present. Hayes discussed at length with his cabinet many of the more difficult questions he faced. Typical were the issues arising during the railroad strike, and the decision to veto the efforts to repeal the Force Act. Today such discussions would be held between the President and top members of his own staff, rather than with the various cabinet officers. The difference is probably due mostly to the tremendous growth of the executive branch, giving cabinet members quite enough to do in the administration of their own departments, and giving the President a circle of trusted advisers with no cabinet rank.

Hayes' administration is notable for the President's championing of executive authority. The tradition of the now-defunct Whig Party, from which he had migrated, favored a weak chief executive. This was quite in keeping with the outlook of its namesake party in England, which championed the cause of Parliament over that of the King. But Hayes, both in his successful use of the veto power and in his insistence on the executive's right to select appointees to important positions in the executive branch, looked toward a more assertive presidency in the future.

THE DEMOCRATS were understandably bitter about the outcome of the election. On March 3, House Democrats passed a resolution declaring Tilden the lawfully elected President, and some of them urged him to take the oath of office on the strength of that resolution. The House would have had a role to play under Article II of the Constitution if the joint session of Congress had not completed its count of the electoral votes. In that event, the election would have been thrown into the House, where, voting by states, the President would have been chosen. But the joint session *did* complete its count, and so the House resolution was of no legal consequence.

The *Washington Union,* Tilden's organ in the nation's capital, suspended publication on March 3, saying:

Fraud has triumphed, and triumphed through the treachery of Democrats. Honest men of irresolute natures and dull perceptions have assisted, but corruption led the way.[2]

The *Cincinnati Enquirer* proclaimed even more emphatically:

It is done. And fitly done in the dark. By the grace of Joe Bradley, R. B. Hayes is "Commissioned" as President, and the monster fraud of the century is consummated.[3]

Some of the more militant elements in the Democratic Party counseled a call to arms; letters from across the country urged such a course. General George McClellan—the Democratic nominee in 1864—gave sympathetic consideration to the possibility of a resort to arms. But Tilden would have none of such a course, and the majority of the Democrats agreed with him. In June 1877, he was tendered a dinner at New York's Manhattan Club, where he expressed these sentiments:

Everybody knows that, after the recent election, the men who were elected by the people as President and Vice President were counted out; and the men who were not elected were counted in and seated. If my voice could reach throughout our country and be heard in its remotest hamlet, I would say: Be of good cheer. The Republic will live. The institutions of our fathers are not to expire in shame. The sovereignty of the people shall be rescued from this peril and re-established.[4]

The strain of the election dispute took a toll on Tilden's health. His left hand was almost useless because of arthritis.

Parkinson's disease made his gait slow and shuffling, and his face had a jaundiced appearance. The summer after the election he vacationed first at Sea Girt, New Jersey, and then in July sailed for Europe with two friends on the liner *Scythia.*

He landed first in Ireland, and then went on to London. He visited the usual tourist spots and sought out some of his English relatives. He then spent a month in Paris. He returned to New York in late October and was immediately plunged into the affairs of the New York State Democratic Party. He had no difficulty refusing to be considered as a candidate for one of the New York seats in the United States Senate.

Although the next presidential election was three years away, it was already on Tilden's mind. He spoke at an elegant dinner given in his honor at Delmonico's restaurant in New York, and occasionally made other speeches expressing his political views.

In the spring of 1878, the Republican minority of the Potter Committee investigated Democratic frauds, and grilled Tilden and his nephew, W. T. Pelton, about a cipher telegram concerning a bribe to one of the returning boards. Tilden appeared before the committee in February 1879:

> He seemed to have aged considerably, and . . . looked quite ill and feeble . . . it was a painful spectacle to see the slow, halting lame walk with which he passed the table and reached his seat. His figure was stiffly drawn up and seemed incapable of bending, as though from a paralytic contraction of the limbs.[5]

Tilden declared that he had no knowledge of Pelton's activities, but Pelton's testimony was quite unsatisfactory, and the matter cast a shadow over Tilden's leadership of the Democratic Party.

But he *was* the leader of that party, and viewed by most of its adherents as the odds-on favorite to be its presidential nominee in 1880.

When virtually the entire Democratic state ticket went down to defeat in the New York election of 1879, Tilden himself began to doubt whether he should be a candidate in 1880. He believed that election as President then would be the ultimate vindication for the denial of the office to him in 1877, but he did not wish to campaign for the nomination. Fan mail and newspaper editorials urged his candidacy, but he remained silent.

Republicans did not remain silent, and were harshly critical. The *New York Times* said:

> The Democratic party does not want any such money grabber, railroad wrecker, and paralytic hypocrite at the helm of the state.[6]

But Democrats continued to support him, though they grew uneasy at his silence as the date of the national convention in June 1880 approached. William C. Whitney, one of his attorneys in the election contest of 1876, was critical:

> One of the peculiar weaknesses of Mr. Tilden as a political leader is that he gives his whole confidence to no one, not even to those on whom he must rely for the execution of his plans. He has reserves in everything he says, he expects his supporters to guess his intentions. And if we do not guess accurately, he is angry. He lost the Presidential seat by just such methods. By withholding his confidence from those who represented his interest in Washington he weakened them with Democratic senators and congressmen who at first were willing, if not anxious, to submit to their lead.[7]

Before the New York delegation left for the national convention in Cincinnati, Tilden told them that he did not want the nomination unless it came to him by unanimous consent. He said he would make his position known in a letter which he would give to his brother, Henry, to take to the convention. The letter spoke of the repugnance he felt at entering an office which would involve "four years of ceaseless toil." But it was not the irrevocable declaration issued by General William T. Sherman at the Republican convention in 1884: "I will not accept if nominated, I will not serve if elected."

After Tilden's letter was made public, some delegates thought it a withdrawal, while others believed it was an invitation to a "draft." Tilden received a few votes on the first ballot, but on the second the convention nominated General Winfield Scott Hancock of Pennsylvania to be the Democratic standard-bearer. Hancock would lose to James A. Garfield in the November election, thus assuring the Republicans of a twenty-four-year tenure in the White House—a record never since achieved by either party.

Four years later Tilden was pressed again to let his hat be placed in the ring for the presidential nomination of his party. But in the intervening years, his physical condition had declined further, and for once he made an unequivocal withdrawal as a possible candidate. He died two years later at the age of seventy-two and was buried in the cemetery of his boyhood home, New Lebanon.

The Republican National Convention of 1880 took an exhausting thirty-six ballots to nominate a presidential candidate to succeed Hayes. One faction of the party—the Stalwarts, led by Hayes' old enemy, Senator Roscoe Conkling—supported none other than Ulysses S. Grant for an unprecedented third term. Opposing them were John Sherman, Hayes' Secretary of the Treasury, and James G. Blaine, Hayes' opponent at the 1876 convention. After a number of ballots, it became obvious that Grant, though having more votes than any of the others, could not win a majority of the delegates. But those opposing Grant appeared unable to unite behind a single candidate. So it went for some thirty ballots, until on the thirty-fourth ballot the Wisconsin delegation cast 16 votes for James A. Garfield. Garfield had not even been nominated, and in fact was managing Sherman's campaign. He rose to a point of order to withdraw his name, but the weary convention nonetheless nominated him only two ballots later.

The omens did not appear favorable to the Republican Party that year. The Democrats now controlled not only the House, but the Senate, and Hancock was one of the heroes of the Battle of Gettysburg. His candidacy would likely neutralize the "bloody shirt" tactics of the Republicans in earlier post–Civil War elections. Hancock, however, was out of his element as a political candidate. The tariff was an issue on which the parties were divided: Republicans favored high tariffs to protect American manufacturers, while the Democrats favored a "tariff for revenue only" to favor American consumers. A famous cartoon drawn by Thomas Nast shows Hancock on a speakers' platform festooned with a large TARIFF FOR REVENUE ONLY banner. Inquiring of the man next to him, Hancock asks, "Who is Tariff, and why is he for Revenue only?" In November, Garfield barely edged out Hancock in the popular vote, but won the electoral vote handily.

President Garfield, like Hayes, would also battle Conkling on patronage matters. First the President refused the senator's demand that the Secretary of the Treasury in his administration come from New York (and thus be subject to the senator's veto under the rubric of "senatorial courtesy"). Their mutual hostility reached a climax when Garfield nominated William H. Robertson, a Conkling enemy, to be collector of the Port of New York.

Justice Stanley Matthews, c. 1870s.

The senator predictably opposed the nomination, but Robertson was nonetheless confirmed by the Senate. Conkling and his ally, Thomas Platt, the junior senator from New York, both resigned their seats to seek reelection by the New York legislature. But that body completed their humiliation by declining to reelect them. Conkling then retired from electoral politics to devote himself to a lucrative private law practice, but sadly, he was a victim of the Great Blizzard of 1888 in New York. Caught downtown, he scorned a cab and walked the entire distance to his house in Gramercy Park. A month later he was dead.

Garfield did not live to enjoy the fruits of his victory. On July 3, 1881, after only four months in office, he was shot in the back by Charles Guiteau, a crazed supporter of the Stalwart wing of the party, in a Washington railroad station on his way to a reunion of his class at Williams College. He lingered for two months, dying in September. He was succeeded by Vice President Chester A. Arthur, whose nomination had been a sop to the antireform Stalwarts. But it was during Arthur's administration that the Pendleton Act—the first major reform of the federal civil service—was enacted by Congress and signed by the President.

AFTER HIS FAILURE to obtain the Republican nomination in 1880, Grant gave up his effort to obtain yet another term as President. He settled in New York City and invested his savings in a brokerage partnership with Ferdinand Ward. Ward's speculations caused the house to fail in 1884, and Grant was left heavily in debt. He wrote magazine articles to keep the wolf from the door, but soon learned that he had incurable throat cancer. He then began to write his *Personal Memoirs,* which were completed only days before his death in 1886. The memoirs were both a critical and a financial success, Mark Twain judging them to be the best military memoirs since Julius Caesar's *Commentaries.*

TOWARD THE END of his administration, Hayes nominated his college friend and political ally Stanley Matthews to be a justice of the Supreme Court. Opponents branded Matthews as a "railroad lawyer" and the Senate, controlled by the Democrats, adjourned without acting on the nomination. But shortly after becoming President, Garfield sent up the nomination, and this time a differently composed Senate confirmed Matthews. He would join a Court on which Miller, Field, and Bradley continued to sit. It was a Court seriously overburdened with cases, a few of great moment, the majority of no consequence to anyone but the litigants.

But Civil Rights cases decided in 1883 were of great moment. Section 5 of the Fourteenth Amendment gives Congress the authority "to enforce, by appropriate legislation, the provisions of this Article." What was "appropriate legislation"? Was Congress limited to simply repeating the provisions of the amendment itself—e.g., "No state shall deprive any person of the equal protection of the laws. . . ."—or could it expand on these provisions? In 1875, it enacted the Civil Rights Act, which was in effect a nineteenth-century "public accommodations" law governing the conduct of private owners of public conveyances, theaters, and inns. The Court held the law unconstitutional, saying that the Fourteenth Amendment was directed to stage actors and not to the conduct of private owners of public accommodations. Miller, Field, and Matthews all joined the opinion of the Court written by Bradley. Only Justice John M. Harlan, appointed to the Court by Hayes, dissented.

But for every case of national importance such as these, there were hundreds that were important only to the parties themselves. This was because one of the grounds on which a party could get his case in federal trial court in the first place, rather than sue in state court, was when the plaintiff was a citizen of one state and the defendant a citizen of another. There was no federal law that governed the merits of these cases, and the federal judge hearing them would simply apply the law of the state in which the court sat. And the losing party had the right to appeal to the United States Supreme Court. As the nation grew, more and more of these "diversity of citizenship" cases were filed in the lower federal courts, and more appeals from their decisions went to the Supreme Court. Often during the 1880s, the Supreme Court would be several years behind in its docket.

For many years, Congress had been urged to create intermediate federal courts of appeals—a line of courts below the Supreme Court which could hear appeals from federal trial courts. But the effort bore no fruit until 1891. In that year, William M. Evarts, who had been Secretary of State in Hayes' cabinet and was now a senator from New York, shepherded through Congress the Evarts Act, which created a system of intermediate courts of appeals. This law gave considerable relief to the Supreme Court.

Justice Matthews died in 1889, after a relatively short time on the Court. Miller died in 1890, Bradley in 1892, and Field in 1899. Each of these three is rated as "near great" in the principal evaluation of Supreme Court justices.[8] They were the three dominant personalities on the post–Civil War Court. As the new century dawned, their successors would have to contend with even more daunting problems than they did.

Each of the participants in the Hayes–Tilden electoral dispute were creatures of the nineteenth century, not only temporally but spiritually. It was the first full century of American nationhood, ushered in by President Thomas Jefferson with the Louisiana Purchase, which extended the western boundary of the United States beyond the Mississippi River. It was ushered out by President William McKinley, with the national boundaries extending not only "from sea to shining sea" but beyond. Travel at its beginning was by horse and sail; at its end it was by rail and steamship. In its midst the nation was rent by a fratricidal civil war.

The Hayes–Tilden electoral dispute was the most contentious political imbroglio of the last half of the century. Thanks to the Electoral Commission, created by Congress and acquiesced to by Hayes and Tilden, the nation avoided serious disturbance or bloodshed and went on about its business. This outcome was a testament to the ability of the American system of government to improvise solutions to even the most difficult and important problems.

— EPILOGUE —

THE OPPROBRIUM WHICH Joseph Bradley endured for his "casting vote" on the Electoral Commission was both unusual and unjustified. But before the Electoral Commission ever began its deliberations, one or more members of the Supreme Court who served on the Commission could expect to be denounced by the party against whom that body ruled. No political event in the United States, then or now, attracts more attention than a presidential election. Millions of people participate every four years; it is foreordained that the candidate of one of the two major political parties will win and the other will lose.

An uncontested result is accepted with more or less good grace; the people have spoken. But if the result is so close as to be disputed, the final outcome of the election will not be so readily accepted. Those who decide the contest will inevitably be subjected to criticism by the party whose candidate is the loser.

No such criticism was uttered against the senators or representatives who sat on the Commission. Each of them, like Sir Joseph Porter in the Gilbert and Sullivan opera *H.M.S. Pinafore,* "always voted at his party's call," and no one was the least bit surprised that they did so. But no such tolerance was granted to the

Supreme Court justices who made up the remaining members of the Commission.

Congress, in establishing the Commission, viewed the members with ambiguity. They were, on the one hand, the men who made possible the whole idea of a commission which would, in practice, have the final say as to the winner of the election. A Republican Senate and a Democratic House could never have agreed on a joint commission of only their members which had the necessary uneven number to decide the question one way or the other. To the evenly divided members of Congress on the Commission there had to be added an uneven number of members from outside Congress. The executive branch, controlled by a Republican President, offered no hope of impartiality. So Congress turned to the judicial branch.

But it did so with great care. It chose the two members of the court who had been appointed by Democratic Presidents—Clifford and Field. They chose a third and fourth member who had been appointed by a Republican President. Of these they had seven to pick from, and they did not go by seniority. Chief Justice Waite had asked not to be considered, and in any event would not have been selected because he was thought to be too close to his fellow Ohioan Hayes. Waite was no fan of Tilden; in October 1876, he wrote to a friend: "I can't help but feel a trust in Providence. It can't be possible that we are to be turned over to the democracy with Sam Tilden at the head. We have not sinned enough for that yet."[1] Congress eventually chose Miller and Strong, and provided that they, together with Clifford and Field, would add a fifth justice.

The tacit understanding was that it would be Davis, regarded as a genuine political Independent. When Davis refused to serve, the four named members chose Bradley. None of these justices were picked for their legal learning, but for their partisan backgrounds. Bradley was the closest substitute for a political Independent as could be had among the remaining members of the Court. So on the one hand the justices were selected to add to the Commission a less obviously partisan aura than the congressional members, but they were named also with a view that the members of the Court were not wholly apolitical.

According to Strong, as related to Garfield, Field was the only one of the five justices who wanted this assignment. And Bradley must have wished it least of all; before the Commission ever sat, he was regarded in the Democratic press as the "casting vote" among its fifteen members. Waite had refused; but could or should Bradley have done likewise?

THE PRACTICE of Supreme Court justices serving in extrajudicial capacities neither began nor ended with the Electoral Commission of 1877. Justices before and after were called upon to broker treaties, sit on committees of investigation, and perform other tasks at the President's behest. Their willingness to do so was partly a product of the Court's increasing importance in the growing nation.

The very first Chief Justice of the Supreme Court, John Jay, undertook an extrajudicial mission at the request of President George Washington. Jay, if not in the front rank of the Founding Fathers—men such as Washington, Jefferson, Hamilton, and Madison—was at least in the second echelon of that distinguished coterie. His family was part of New York's colonial aristocracy. He practiced his profession without public recognition until 1774, when he was elected one of New York's delegates to the first Continental Congress in Philadelphia. At the beginning of the Revolutionary War, he was active in a state convention which instructed the New York delegation in Philadelphia to sign the Declaration of Independence.

He later became the state's Chief Justice at a difficult time; New York City was occupied by British troops after the Battle of Brooklyn in the summer of 1776, and other parts of the state were controlled by England. Jay went on to serve briefly as president of the Continental Congress, as its minister to Spain, and as one of the negotiators of the Treaty of Paris which ended the Revolutionary War in 1783. He was named Secretary of Foreign Affairs in the next year and served in that post until the ratification of the Constitution in 1789. He played an important part in persuading the New York State legislature to ratify that document, which it did by the narrow margin of three votes.

Washington appointed Jay Chief Justice of the newly created United States Supreme Court in 1789, and the Court met for the first time early in 1790. There were few appeals for the Court to hear, and so most of the justices' time was spent "riding circuit"—sitting as a trial judge in different cities within the geographical area assigned to them.

Disputes between Great Britain and the United States came to the forefront during Washington's second term. The British had never relinquished their forts in the area of the Great Lakes, and their naval vessels continued to "impress" American seamen for service in the Royal Navy. On the other hand, British and Loyalist creditors whose rights were protected by the Treaty of Paris were given the runaround when they sought relief against American debtors. In 1794, Washington asked Jay to serve as a special envoy to Great Britain in order to settle these disputes.

Jay by no means wanted this appointment. Because of the deep division in the country between those who preferred negotiation and those who preferred war, he believed that no emissary could negotiate a treaty without seriously damaging his reputation and career. Yet the United States was in no position to wage war successfully against Great Britain; it had no navy and scarcely any army. Jay wrote to his wife:

> No appointment ever operated more unpleasantly upon me; but the public considerations which were urged, and the manner in which it was pressed, strongly impressed me with a conviction that to refuse it would be to desert my duty for the sake of my ease and domestic concerns and comforts.[2]

Interestingly enough, he does not mention the effect that his absence on such a mission might have on the Supreme Court. He accepted the post and was in England for a year. The treaty he negotiated settled some, but not all, of the disputes between the two countries. Great Britain agreed to abandon her western posts in 1796 but refused compensation for their present occupancy. She also granted very limited access for American commercial shipping to the British West Indies, which had been a mainstay of American commerce before the Revolution. Britain refused to budge on the impressment of American seamen, but commissions were appointed to adjudicate private claims of Americans against Britain, and private claims of British citizens against the United States.

The Jay Treaty aroused a storm of criticism when its provisions were published in the United States. Jay was burned in effigy by angry crowds of Jeffersonian Republicans, and the treaty was criticized by some Federalists as well. But most historians have come to regard it as the best that could be had for the United States.

Upon Jay's return from England, he was elected Governor of New York and resigned the Chief Justiceship to accept that office. This choice on his part must be viewed in the light of the times in which he acted. Less than a decade after its creation, the Supreme Court had gotten off to a very slow start. It decided on the average of ten cases each year in its first decade of existence. When Jay resigned the Chief Justiceship, the Court was not generally regarded as a truly coequal branch of a tripartite federal government. It achieved that status under Chief Justice John Marshall, who served from 1801 to 1835.

Jay served six years as Governor of New York and lived for nearly thirty more. Upon his resignation as Chief Justice, Washington nominated John Rutledge of South Carolina to succeed him. Ironically, and unfortunately for Rutledge, he had made a speech in his home state denouncing the Jay Treaty; the Federalist-dominated Senate refused to confirm him in December 1795, so he served for only a few months under a recess appointment.

Washington then nominated Oliver Ellsworth of Connecticut. He, too, would be sent on a foreign mission while holding that office—by John Adams, who succeeded Washington in 1797. Adams named Ellsworth as one of a three-man delegation to go to Paris and negotiate an end to the "undeclared war" between France and the United States. Like Jay, he was gone for a year and does not seem to have been greatly missed by his colleagues on the Court. In the fall of 1800 he fell ill in Paris and sent his resignation to President Adams.

NEARLY EIGHT DECADES passed between the time of Ellsworth's resignation and the service of the five Supreme Court justices on the Electoral Commission in 1877. Twenty years after that, Chief Justice Melville W. Fuller was asked on two occasions to serve in an extrajudicial office.

Fuller was born in 1833 and lived until he was a young adult in Augusta, Maine. He then pulled up stakes and headed west for the raw, bustling city of Chicago. The city was growing by leaps and bounds because of its location at the foot of Lake Michigan; it would eventually become the center of the largest railroad network in the country.

Fuller took up the practice of law, and in time rose to the top of the Chicago bar. He was also active in Democratic politics, serving a term in the legislature and as a delegate to a state constitutional convention. It was this party activity which lead to his acquaintance with Grover Cleveland of New York. During Cleveland's first term as President, Chief Justice Waite died in the spring of 1888, and Cleveland nominated Fuller to succeed him.

Fuller had not been in uniform in the Civil War, and during his one term in the Illinois legislature he joined with other Democrats in opposing some of the war measures proposed by Richard Yates, the Republican Governor. As a result, a number of Republican senators stood against his confirmation as Chief Justice twenty-five years later. They printed a pamphlet which concluded:

> The records of the Illinois legislature of 1863 are black with Mr. Fuller's unworthy and unpatriotic conduct. . . . They cannot be answered by fond exclamations about "Mel Fuller" or that he was a Douglas man or that "Maine cannot produce copperheads." . . . Let us hope that no Senator . . . whether he calls himself a Democrat or Republican will tolerate a copperhead as Chief Justice of the United States.[3]

Nearly four months after his nomination, the Senate confirmed Fuller by a vote of 41 to 20.

The Court over which Fuller presided was a markedly different institution from that of John Jay's time. Instead of deciding ten cases per year, it was reviewing 200 to 300 cases annually and still falling steadily behind in its docket. A case might wait as long as three years to be decided. This congestion was alleviated by the enactment of the Circuit Court of Appeals Act of 1891, which created intermediate federal courts of appeals in different parts of the country. But the Court still had to decide upwards of 200 cases every year. And it was in this context that the Venezuela Boundary Dispute arose in 1896.

The boundary between British Guiana and Venezuela had been contested for a number of years. But President Cleveland invoked the Monroe Doctrine to pressure Great Britain into entering an agreement to arbitrate the dispute. Under the treaty thus negotiated, one of the arbitrators was to be designated by the President of Venezuela, one by the justices of the United States Supreme Court, and two by the British Privy Council; these four were to select a fifth member of the tribunal. The President of Venezuela appointed Fuller, and the Supreme Court selected Associate Justice David J. Brewer, a nephew of Stephen J. Field. Frederick DeMartins, a Russian jurist, was chosen as the fifth member of the panel. But Fuller would regret his acceptance of the appointment when the volumes of evidence submitted to the tribunal poured in. That body was originally scheduled to meet in Paris in the middle of the October 1898 term of the Supreme Court, but Fuller wrote to his English counterparts that neither he nor Justice Brewer could possibly go to Europe before the Court adjourned in the late spring. And so they would both spend the summer of 1899 abroad.

At roughly the same time, the Spanish-American War broke out. The United States had long sympathized with the Cubans, who were harshly treated by their Spanish overlords. In early

1898, the U.S. battleship *Maine* was blown up in Havana Harbor. Suspicion that the blast had been intentionally caused by Spanish officials fueled war fever in the United States to cries of "Remember the Maine." Congress declared war in March 1898, but the war was short-lived. The U.S. Army in Cuba, and the U.S. Navy there and in the Philippines, completely crushed the Spanish armed forces. In August, President William McKinley, who had succeeded Cleveland in the previous year, sent Fuller the following telegram at his summer home in Sorrento, Maine:

IT WOULD GIVE ME SPECIAL PLEASURE IF YOU WOULD PERMIT ME TO CONSIDER YOU FOR MEMBERSHIP ON THE PEACE COMMIS- SION. WIRE ANSWER. WILLIAM MCKINLEY.

Fuller first wired, and then wrote McKinley in detail of his reasons for declining:

My Dear Mr. President:

Your telegram of yesterday came during my absence and I did not receive it until later in the afternoon. This led to haste in my reply and I answered as I did partly from a feeling that perhaps it might be a duty to accept if you thought fit to tender the appointment and partly out of my personal regard for you if perchance you were embarrassed as to a choice. But on reflection I became absolutely con- vinced that the path of duty laid distinctly the other way and accordingly telegraphed you this morning. I would have done so last night but the office was closed.

   I am as you are aware one of the arbitrators under the Anglo-Venezuelan treaty and although the hearing will doubtless not be had until next summer, either Mr. Justice Brewer or myself or both of us may be compelled to go over to Paris in February to attend the organization of the tribunal. At the time I assented to the wish that I should accept the position it seemed best that I should do so but I have become satisfied since that I was mistaken in the view that I then entertained.

My duty to the country lies in the discharge of my duty to the Court over which I preside and the labors of the Court are, as you know arduous and many matters of detail necessarily devolve upon the Chief Justice. Nothing but some imperative exigency ought to be allowed to interfere in any way with the conduct of the business that we are appointed to perform and I am quite sure that the Chief Justice should not take on any additional burden. . . .[4]

Fuller's reasons, it may be noted, were quite different from those advanced by Jay a century earlier. Fuller rightly anticipated no harm to his reputation in serving on the Venezuela Boundary Commission, whose actions were of little interest to most of his countrymen. The Peace Commission's work, ending the Spanish-American War, was of course of more interest to them, but negotiating a treaty with a badly beaten enemy carried few of the risks that Jay's parley with Great Britain carried for him. Fuller's concern was entirely for the work of the Court, which he felt would suffer if his time were spent elsewhere. The role of the Chief Justice at the end of the nineteenth century was much more demanding than a century earlier.

Not until the mid-twentieth century was a member of the Supreme Court again called upon to undertake a significant extrajudicial mission, and this time the issue at hand was the United States' preparedness for World War II. In July 1941, Japan announced that it had assumed a protectorate over all of what was then French Indo-China. President Franklin D. Roosevelt then froze Japan's assets in the United States, and Britain and the Netherlands did the same, cutting off Japan's purchases of oil, rubber, and scrap iron. In October, the Japanese cabinet, headed by Prince Konoye, who wished to conciliate the Allies, fell. He was succeeded by Hideki Tojo, representing the more aggressive views of the Japanese military. Negotiations were then opened between Japan and the United States, but the parties were so far apart that there was no real hope of a successful conclusion.

On November 27, the top Army and Navy officials in Washington sent messages to General Walter Short, the Army commander in Hawaii, and Admiral Husband E. Kimmel, the Navy commander there. These messages related that negotiations between the United States and Japan were going nowhere, and Japanese military attacks against the Philippines, Thailand, or the Kra Peninsula were expected because of the movements of Japanese troops and naval task forces.

The measures taken in response to this warning would become a matter of controversy. On November 26, a Japanese task force consisting of 2 battleships, 2 heavy cruisers, 11 destroyers, and 6 aircraft carriers carrying over 400 planes started from its staging area in the Kurile Islands off Japan for its destination: the U.S. naval base at Pearl Harbor in Hawaii. At 7:55 a.m. on December 7, the Japanese planes bombed and torpedoed U.S. planes and battleships located there.

More than 2,000 American troops and civilians were killed in the raid, 140 planes destroyed on the ground, 2 battleships sunk, and 4 others damaged. In his radio broadcast the following day asking Congress for a declaration of war, President Roosevelt referred to December 7 as a "date that would live in infamy."

The response of the American public in the immediate aftermath of the attack on Pearl Harbor was outrage against Japan mixed with dismay at the lack of preparedness of the United States forces at Pearl Harbor and in the Philippines. Senator Robert Taft of Ohio, a leader of the isolationist wing of the Republican Party, called for a congressional investigation of the situation, and several of his colleagues joined him. Roosevelt was alarmed by the prospect of such an inquiry; release of the cable traffic would alert the Japanese to the fact that the United States had broken the Japanese code, and any open-ended probe could provide fodder for his political opponents in the 1942 elections.

The President turned to Justice Owen Roberts to head an investigating commission. Roberts had been a highly successful Philadelphia lawyer, and the special prosecutor in the Teapot Dome Scandal in the mid-twenties; he was appointed to the Supreme Court by Herbert Hoover in 1930. Roosevelt issued an executive order on December 18 appointing Roberts as chairman and four senior military officers as members "to ascertain and report the facts relating to the attack made by Japanese armed forces upon the territory of Hawaii on December 7, 1941.

> The purposes of the required inquiry and report are to provide bases for sound decisions whether any derelictions of duty or errors of judgment on the part of the United States Army or Navy personnel contributed to such successes as were achieved by the enemy on the occasion. . . ."[5]

The Commission went to work immediately, meeting in Washington on December 18 through 20, on the last date leaving for Honolulu, where they arrived on December 22. A series of meetings was held at various places in Hawaii—over a period of three weeks. In mid-January, the members returned to Washington and held regular sessions for the next week. In all, the Commission examined nearly 150 witnesses and received numerous documents. All persons, military or civilian, who were thought to have knowledge of relevant events were subpoenaed. In addition, the Commission issued a public notice inviting all persons residing on Oahu who might have useful knowledge to appear, and a number did so. On January 23, the Commission submitted a twenty-one-page report to the President. The report is surprisingly readable for a government document. Its critical findings were these.

First, in January 1941, just about the time that Admiral Kimmel and General Short assumed their respective commands in Hawaii, the Secretary of the Navy wrote the Secretary of War that increasing friction between Japan and the United States had prompted a review of security measures for the fleet while it was in Pearl Harbor. The letter pointed out that "if war eventuates with Japan, it is believed easily possible that hostilities would be instigated by a surprise attack on the fleet or the naval base at Pearl Harbor." It urged coordination of Navy and Army efforts to ensure preparedness. Kimmel and Short each received a copy of the letter.

Second, on November 24, 1941, the Chief of Naval Operations sent a message to Kimmel saying that the Navy Department thought a surprise aggressive movement by Japan in any direction, most likely on the Philippines or Guam, was a possibility.

Third, on November 27 the Army Chief of Staff informed General Short that negotiations with Japan were ending, and that hostilities on its part were momentarily possible.

Fourth, that same day, the Chief of Naval Operations sent a message to the Commander of the Pacific Fleet that Japan was expected to make an aggressive move within the next few days, and that an amphibious expedition against either the Philippines, Thailand, or the Kra Peninsula was likely.

Fifth, Article XI of the Roberts Report stated:

> At about noon, eastern standard time (6:30 a.m. Honolulu time), December 7, an additional warning message, indicating an almost immediate break in relations between the United States and Japan, was dispatched by the Chief of Staff after conference with the Chief of Naval Operations, for the information of responsible Army and Navy commanders. Every effort was made to have the message reach Hawaii in the briefest possible time, but due to conditions beyond the control of anyone concerned the delivery of this urgent message was delayed until after the attack.

The Commission found that the failure of Kimmel and Short to confer with each other about joint defense plans in the light of repeated warnings was a dereliction of duty. Each commander had committed errors of judgment in not recognizing the seriousness of the situation.

Kimmel in particular—and after he died, his descendants—carried on a campaign to rehabilitate himself. He succeeded in getting the "dereliction of duty" changed to "errors of judgment." But numerous other critics of the Roberts Commission Report have sought, not so much to vindicate Kimmel and Short, but to implicate the Washington high command, from the President on down. The more extreme of these critics seek to show that Roosevelt not only provoked the attack on Pearl Harbor, but actually welcomed it, and, indeed, perhaps had advance knowledge of it. That the measures taken by his administration in the summer of 1941 ended the hope of any reconciliation with Japan is doubtless true, but it is a big and unjustifiable leap from that proposition to the conclusion that FDR knew of the impending attack on Pearl Harbor and failed to alert the U.S. commanders in Hawaii.

A more reasonable school of critics faults the military command in Washington for having itself failed—in the face of an intercepted Japanese cable instructing Japan's emissaries in Washington to break diplomatic relations, and its embassy to burn all documents—to immediately warn the commanders in Pearl Harbor of the sharply increased likelihood of war—not at some time in the near future, but *now.* An Army board investigating Pearl Harbor several years later concluded that "[General George Marshall failed] to get to General Short on the evening of December 6th and the early morning of December 7th, the critical information indicating an almost immediate break with Japan, though there was ample time to have accomplished this."[6]

That the Roberts Commission, including four high-ranking military officers in its membership of five, and deliberating during the weeks immediately following Pearl Harbor, would thus criticize the Army Chief of Staff was unlikely, to say the least. But the very summary nature of the clean bill of health given to the Washington brass by paragraph 11 of the report, quoted above, saying that "due to conditions beyond the control of anyone concerned the delivery of this urgent message was delayed," does not seem to have been the subject of any careful investigation by the Commission and probably should have been omitted.

Justice Roberts did not sit during the Supreme Court's argument session in January 1942. Harlan F. Stone, who had become Chief Justice six months earlier, expressed his irritation at Roberts' absence and at Justice James F. Byrnes' spending time at the White House consulting on wartime economic planning. He wrote his son:

> I am struggling along with the work of the Court as best I can, with one and a half men away. . . . Roberts has returned from Hawaii, but I think he is still busy preparing his report. I am hoping that we shall get him back on the job soon.[7]

It was to be a bad year for Stone. In June he would read in the press of Associate Justice Frank Murphy's receiving a commission as a lieutenant colonel in the Army, and there would soon be complaints from members of Congress as to the legality of Murphy's holding two federal positions. A month later, he would confront the issue of extrajudicial duties directly. Roosevelt asked him to conduct an inquiry into the problem of rubber production for the war effort. The need for such an inquiry was prompted by a politically charged dispute both within the administration and in Congress as to the best way to produce synthetic rubber. Stone replied to the President three days later:

> Dear Mr. President:
>
> I have your letter of the 17th inst. Personal and patriotic considerations alike afford powerful incentives for my wish to comply with your request that I assist you in arriving at some solution of the pending rubber problem. But most anxious, not to say painful, reflection has led me to the conclusion that I cannot rightly yield to my desire to render for you a service which as a private citizen I should not only feel bound to do but one which I should undertake with zeal and enthusiasm. . . .
>
> A judge, and especially the Chief Justice, cannot engage

in political debate or make public defense of his acts. When his action is judicial he may always rely upon the support of the defined record upon which his action is based and of the opinion in which he and his associates unite as stating the ground of decision. But when he participates in the action of the executive or legislative departments of government he is without those supports. He exposes himself to attack and indeed invites it, which because of his peculiar situation inevitably impairs his value as a judge and the appropriate influence of his office.

We must not forget that it is the judgment of history that two of my predecessors, Jay and Ellsworth, failed in the obligations of their office and impaired their legitimate influence by participation in executive action in the negotiation of treaties. True, they repaired their mistake in part by resigning their commissions before returning to their judicial duties, but it is not by mere chance that every Chief Justice since has confined his activities strictly to the performance of his judicial duties. . . .

Finally, in October 1942, Justice Byrnes resigned from the Court to devote all of his time to the newly created post of director of economic stabilization. Stone, seldom effusive in his praise, wrote, "I am sorry to lose you from the Court, but I'm glad you can make up your mind whether you want to be a judge or something else."

LESS THAN three years later, the issue of Supreme Court justices taking on extrajudicial duties presented itself in as sharp a focus as can be imagined. Roosevelt died at Warm Springs, Georgia, on April 12, 1945. He was succeeded by his Vice President, Harry S Truman. The allies in Europe were sweeping to victory—V-E Day was less than a month away. In late April, Truman asked Supreme Court Associate Justice Robert Jackson to take on the job of chief U.S. prosecutor before an international tribunal to try high German officials accused of war crimes. Within days, Jackson accepted the position with conditions which proved satisfactory to the President. By an executive order dated May 2, Truman appointed Jackson as chief prosecutor.

Robert H. Jackson was born in 1892 and grew up in Jamestown, New York. He was active in the state Democratic Party and, as a result, became a friend of Roosevelt. After Roosevelt became President in 1933, he brought Jackson to Washington as general counsel to the then Bureau of Internal Revenue. Jackson rose rapidly in the executive hierarchy, serving as assistant attorney general in the Anti-Trust Division of the Justice Department, as solicitor general, and finally as Attorney General. When Roosevelt elevated Stone to the Chief Justiceship in 1941, he appointed Jackson as an associate justice.

Jackson took on an enormous responsibility, not just as an advocate before the tribunal, but also as a de facto ambassador and as administrator. There had never been such a tribunal before. The United States would prosecute—and judge—along with its wartime allies Britain, Russia, and France. Agreement as to which country would do what, and when, had to be negotiated. A sizable and highly competent staff had to be assembled on short notice, to depart for war-torn Europe for an indefinite period of time.

Jackson made the first of several trips to Europe in late May to discuss preliminary matters. This was before the age of jet propulsion, and travel was by propeller plane. These planes could not cross the Atlantic Ocean without refueling. Thus a flight from Washington or New York to Paris, like Jackson's, would stop first at Newfoundland, and then in the Azores, before the final leg to its destination. In Paris, agreements were duly negotiated among the Allies over the summer. Nuremberg, Germany, was designated as the place for the trials to be held.

These trials began in late November 1945, and Jackson was the first to make an opening statement to the tribunal. He spoke for an entire day and won high praise from American reporters covering the event. Several months later, he undertook the principal cross-examination of Hermann Göring, the highest-ranking German official on trial. Press reviews of this effort were mixed. After all the evidence was in, in late July, Jackson also made the first of the closing speeches for the prosecution. On August 31, the tribunal recessed to consider the cases against the defendants. Its judgment was handed down a month later: of the twenty-two defendants, twelve were sentenced to hang, three to life imprisonment, four to terms ranging from ten to twenty years, and three were acquitted.

Jackson understandably regarded his participation in the Nuremberg Trials as the crowning achievement of his career. Telford Taylor, one of the other U.S. prosecutors, evaluated Jackson's performance there in these words:

> In concluding this discussion, I must recur to the unique and vital role played by Justice Jackson. He made mistakes and some bad ones, but there was much more to the Nuremberg case than legal disquisition or cross-examination. Two other things were vital: passion and eloquence. More than any other man of that period, Jackson worked and wrote with deep passion and spoke in winged words. There was no one else who could have done that half as well as he.[8]

Criticism of the Nuremberg Trials focused on two issues. The first was whether a Supreme Court justice should participate as a prosecutor in such a trial. The Republican-controlled Senate Judiciary Committee in 1947 opined

> that the practice of using federal judges for non-judicial activities is undesirable. The practice holds great danger of working in diminution of the prestige of the judiciary. It is a deterrent to the proper functioning of the judicial branch of the government.[9]

The second issue was whether or not this sort of trial—not only the prosecutors, but also the judges coming from the victors—would be in fact if not in form a "kangaroo court." But this criticism softened as the court amassed evidence of the evil intentions and deeds of many of the defendants, and also because three of the defendants were acquitted. Legal scholars also questioned whether the whole idea of such a trial where there was no existing body of law did not violate the principle embodied in the ex post facto prohibition in the United States Constitution. That provision requires that before criminal liability may attach to a person for a particular act, a law making the conduct criminal must have been on the books at the time he committed the act.

Some of Jackson's own colleagues joined in the criticism. Justice William O. Douglas (between Jackson and whom no love was lost) opined in memoirs published many years later:

> [Jackson] was gone a whole year, and in his absence we sat as an eight-man Court. I thought at the time he accepted the job that it was a gross violation of separation of powers to put a Justice in charge of an executive function. I thought, and I

think Stone and Black agreed, that if Bob did that, he should resign. Moreover, some of us—particularly Stone, Black, Murphy and I—thought that the Nuremberg Trials were unconstitutional *by American standards.*[10]

Whatever the merit of these objections, the Nuremberg Trials were surely superior to the summary court-martial proceedings favored by some members of the administration. In private, Stone was vituperative; writing to a longtime friend, he said:

Jackson is away conducting his high-grade lynching party in Nuremberg. . . . I don't mind what he does to the Nazis, but I hate to see the pretense that he is running a court and proceeding according to common law. This is a little too sanctimonious a fraud to meet my old-fashioned ideas.[11]

Stone's biographer, Altheus T. Mason, sums up Stone's more considered view this way:

For Stone, Justice Jackson's participation in the Nuremberg Trials combined three major sources of irritation: this approval in principle of non-judicial work, strong objection to the trials on legal and political grounds, the inconvenience and increased burden of work entailed. Even if the Chief Justice had wholly approved the trials themselves, he would have disapproved Jackson's role in them. If he had felt differently about the task in which Jackson was engaged, he might have been somewhat less annoyed by his colleague's absence.[12]

Stone's criticism of Jackson's taking the job of prosecutor has considerable justification. Jackson had been gone for one entire term of the Court, and his colleagues had to take up the slack by dividing up what would have been his share of the opinions. In any case in which the eight justices were equally divided, the Court had two alternatives, neither of which was attractive. It could simply hand down a one-sentence order announcing that the decision of the lower court was affirmed by an equally divided vote, an order which by custom says nothing about the governing law. The same issue, which presumably the Court thought important enough to review, would have to await decision until another case in which all nine members of the Court were present. The other alternative was to simply set the case down for reargument when the ninth justice returned.

It is difficult not to sympathize with both Jackson's and Stone's views. Jackson, speaking to the New York State Bar Association in 1947, said that his Nuremberg role "was the supremely interesting and important work of my life and an experience which would be unique in the life of any lawyer."[13] One of Stone's complaints was that he first learned of Jackson's acceptance as prosecutor when it was announced by President Truman. One would think that Jackson would have at least consulted Stone before taking the job; not that Stone had any authority to forbid his taking it, but that advance notice would make it more palatable to Stone.

IN THE PRESIDENTIAL ELECTION of 1952, Republican candidate Dwight D. Eisenhower defeated Adlai Stevenson, the Democratic candidate, ending twenty years of drought for his party. The next year Fred M. Vinson, who succeeded Harlan Stone as Chief Justice, died, and Eisenhower appointed Earl Warren of California to succeed him.

Warren grew up in Bakersfield, California, and after graduating from law school at the University of California became the prosecuting attorney in Oakland. From that post, he was first elected attorney general of the state and then three times Governor of California. Warren had little experience as a practicing lawyer, and he came to the Court at a very difficult time. It was to hear the school desegregation case, *Brown v. Board of Education,* argued for the second time. The Court had been sharply divided after the first argument, but Warren throughout the term persuaded initially reluctant colleagues to make his opinion for the Court in the case unanimous. It held that legally enforced racial segregation in public schools violated the Equal Protection Clause of the United States Constitution.

In 1960, Democratic presidential candidate John F. Kennedy narrowly defeated Republican candidate Richard Nixon. Kennedy was the first Roman Catholic and the second-youngest person to occupy the nation's highest office. He and his attractive wife brought a sense of youth and élan to Washington. The nation was stunned when on November 22, 1963, he was assassinated while riding in a motorcade in Dallas. Lee Harvey Oswald was arrested the same day and charged with the crime. Grief turned to amazement when Oswald, being televised in the custody of the Dallas police, was shot and killed by a local bar owner named Jack Ruby. Rumors of all sorts began to fly.

A week after the assassination, Chief Justice Warren was contacted by the deputy attorney general and the solicitor general to inquire if he would serve as chairman of a bipartisan commission that the new President, Lyndon B. Johnson, would create to investigate the assassination. Warren tells of his initial response in his *Memoirs:*

> I told them I thought the President was wise in having such a commission, but that I was not available for service on it.

Because of past experiences of that kind in the history of the Court, we had discussed the propriety of taking on extrajudicial appointments and, although we had never voted on it, I was sure that every member of the Court was of the opinion that such appointments were not in its best interests. I told Katzenbach and Cox that I had more than once expressed myself to that effect for several reasons. First, it is not in the spirit of constitutional separation of powers to have a member of the Supreme Court serve on a presidential commission; second, it would distract a Justice from the work of the Court, which had a heavy docket; and, third, it was impossible to foresee what litigation such a commission might spawn, with resulting disqualification of the Justice from sitting in such cases.[14]

Later the same day, Warren was summoned to the White House to have his arm twisted by Johnson. The President was successful. He said to the Chief Justice:

"You were a soldier in World War I, but there was nothing you could do in that uniform comparable to what you can do for your country in this hour of trouble." He then told me how serious were the rumors floating around the world. The gravity of the situation was such that it might lead us into war, he said, and, if so, it might be a nuclear war. . . . I then said, "Mr. President, if the situation is that serious, my personal views do not count. I will do it."[15]

The Warren Commission included a bipartisan group of well-known current or former public officials. The following September, the Commission produced an 888-page summary of its findings known as "the Warren Report." The Commission concluded that Oswald acted alone in killing the President and that Ruby acted alone in killing Oswald.

Although the Warren Report was supported by twenty-six volumes of evidence and testimony, from almost the moment it was issued it came under wide criticism from a variety of sources. Hundreds of books and articles have attempted to prove that the Warren Commission got it wrong and that President Kennedy's assassination was the result of a conspiracy. The alleged participants in the conspiracy range from the CIA and the FBI to anti-Castro Cuban groups to the Mafia. The 1991 movie *JFK,* loosely based upon New Orleans District Attorney Jim Garrison's prosecution of Clay Shaw for conspiracy, promoted the theory that Shaw, who was a respected New Orleans businessman, David Ferrie, an airplane charter pilot, and Oswald were part of a conspiracy orchestrated by the military and the CIA.

The Warren Commission concluded that Kennedy was struck by two bullets, both fired from above and behind the President. This conclusion was based in large part on the testimony of the doctors who treated him in Dallas and the doctors who performed the autopsy at the Bethesda Naval Medical Center. The Commission did not consider the autopsy X-rays and photographs (although Warren himself reviewed the photographs) because they planned to make all of the evidence reviewed by the Commission public and did not want to release gruesome photographs of the President. Much criticism of the Warren Commission was generated by its failure to use the photographs and X-rays to evaluate the testimony of the doctors. This failure was seen as either a purposeful cover-up or shoddy investigation. And the secrecy surrounding the autopsy photographs and X-rays fueled conspiracy theorists, with allegations of doctored photographs and X-rays still being made today.

The Commission's conclusion that there was only one gunman and that there were only two bullets that struck the President and Texas Governor John Connally, who was also injured, evolved into what has been dubbed the "single bullet" theory. The Commission found that the first bullet that struck President Kennedy entered his upper back, exited through his neck, then struck Governor Connally, who was sitting in front of the President, entered just below Connally's right armpit, exited his right chest, struck and shattered his right wrist, and ended up in his left thigh.

The existence of a film taken by amateur photographer Abraham Zapruder, reinforced skepticism in the Warren Commission's conclusions. The film shows the President's head being thrown backward as if a bullet had struck him in the front of the head. Added to this were the witnesses who claimed to have heard shots or seen a puff of smoke coming from the "grassy knoll" in front of the President.

Amid the mounting criticism of the report, Chief Justice Warren refused to respond or defend it, simply telling his staff that it spoke for itself. In 1967, according to a Gallup poll, 60 percent of Americans doubted that Oswald was the lone gunman in Dallas.

In September 1976, the House Select Committee on Assassinations was established to investigate the murders of President Kennedy and the Reverend Martin Luther King, Jr. The committee's report on the Kennedy assassination confirmed the conclusions of the Warren Commission that President Kennedy was struck by two shots fired by Oswald from the Texas School Book Depository building and that the second shot killed him. It concluded, however, that President Kennedy "was probably assassinated as a result of a conspiracy," that the Warren Commission was too definitive in its findings, and that it failed adequately to investigate the possibility of a conspiracy.

IF WE STEP back to review the examples of Supreme Court justices performing extrajudicial duties, they are obviously different as to the time at which they occurred, the nature of the assignment, and the effect that the assignment would have on the work of the Court. It would be unthinkable now for a Chief Justice to leave not only the Court, but the United States, for an entire year to undertake a diplomatic mission in a foreign country, as both Jay and Ellsworth did. But the Court was a totally different institution then than it was even a century later. And in a brand-new nation of only 3 or 4 million people, there was much less choice available to the President than there would be at later times.

Passing over the justices who served on the Electoral Commission of 1877 for the moment, Fuller's acceptance of the Venezuela Boundary arbitration seems debatable. He was appointed by the President of Venezuela, so it might have been diplomatically difficult to refuse. Fuller spent an entire summer at the task, but it was while the Court was in recess; the result of the arbitration was not apt to be controversial in the United States. One suspects that by the time Fuller turned down McKinley's request to serve on the Peace Commission, he already had second thoughts about the Venezuela arbitration. And he was surely right in declining that appointment.

Owen Roberts' service on the Pearl Harbor Commission required that he miss one of the seven monthly argument sessions which take place during the annual term of the Court. The Commission served an important national purpose—to examine as soon as possible whether the loss of life, ships, and planes at Pearl Harbor might have been at least partially preventable. The work of the Commission could not have been postponed to the summer recess of the Court and still accomplish its desired purpose. The report was of great interest to the American people and did generate controversy in later years.

Stone was obviously correct in declining Roosevelt's request to referee a politically charged dispute about how best to produce synthetic rubber. He had no special knowledge of the subject matter, and whatever his conclusion, it would be politically attacked by one side or the other. As a sitting judge, he would not be in a position to publicly defend it.

Jackson's service as Chief U.S. counsel at Nuremberg was the most harmful in its effect on the Court of any extrajudicial task in modern times; he missed an entire term of the Court. His stature as a jurist undoubtedly contributed to the success of the Nuremberg Trials; but over and above that, this role was "right up his alley"—the use of the spoken and written word—in a way that it would not have been for his colleagues or most other judges. There was also an element here that was not present in the other cases described: it was an advocate's dream. Earl Warren, for example, accepted the chairmanship of the Warren Commission only after extraordinary importuning from President Johnson; there is surely no reason to believe that he wanted the job. Jackson very much desired the position he was offered; the temptation to which he succumbed was far greater than in the other cases. He accepted with alacrity, thereby recognizing the possibilities of the tendered position, but also showing little regard for the effect of his acceptance on his colleagues and on the Court itself.

Turning back now to the justices who served on the Electoral Commission of 1877, should they have accepted this assignment? Even before the first meeting of the Commission, each one of them could surely see that its work would be the subject of violent and prolonged criticism from the party against whom it ruled. They would be deciding not just who was at fault at Pearl Harbor, or who assassinated John F. Kennedy; they would be deciding who would be the next President of the United States. Members of the Court, if not the Court itself, would participate in a decision that had enormous political consequences.

But the consequences of refusal would be equally momentous. Until Congress passed the law creating the Electoral Commission, realistic threats of violence—of armed partisans marching on Washington—were heard from several quarters. It was evident that Congress, divided as it was, could not resolve the dispute by itself. But because public opinion gradually came to prefer a negotiated settlement, Congress managed to enact a measure which was grudgingly accepted by most of the partisans on each side. The law expressly named four of the justices who were to be members; if they refused, the law contained no authorization for selection of any alternates. The Commission would be a dead letter, and the country would be thrown back to some form of either violence or political Russian roulette.

Critics, including Earl Warren, have expressed the view that the justices serving on the Electoral Commission demeaned the Court. But here one must be reminded of Lincoln's comment when he was accused of acting contrary to the Constitution: "Shall I save the Constitution, but lose the nation?" Four of the five justices, according to Garfield, would rather this cup had passed from them, but the consequences of their refusal would have been grave, if not entirely foreseeable. They may have tarnished the reputation of the Court, but they may also have saved the nation from, if not widespread violence, a situation fraught with combustible uncertainty. In the view of this author, in accepting membership on the Commission, they did the right thing.

Notes

CHAPTER ONE

1. Quoted in Russell F. Weigley, ed., *Philadelphia* (New York, London: W. W. Norton, 1982), p. 466.

2. Paul Leland Haworth, *The Hayes-Tilden Election* (Indianapolis: Bobbs-Merrill Co., 1906), p. 5.

3. Jean Edward Smith, *Grant* (New York: Simon & Schuster, 2001), p. 548.

4. William Harlan Hale, *Horace Greeley* (New York: Harper & Brothers, 1950), p. 337.

5. Geoffrey Perret, *Ulysses S. Grant* (New York: Random House, 1997), p. 421.

6. But finally, in their 1896 convention, the Democrats would nominate William Jennings Bryan for President on a platform calling for unlimited coinage of silver—another inflationary device—thereby parting company not only with the Republicans, but with the just-concluding presidency of Democrat Grover Cleveland.

7. Smith, p. 586.

CHAPTER TWO

1. Ari Hoogenboom, *Rutherford B. Hayes* (Lawrence: University Press of Kansas, 1995), p. 106.

2. Ibid., p. 117.

3. Ibid., pp. 187–88.

4. *Congressional Globe,* April 30, 1866, p. 2299.

5. *Dictionary of American Biography,* vol. XIII, p. 264.

6. *Official Proceedings of the Republican National Convention, 1876,* p. 296.

7. *Chicago Times,* June 16, 1876.

8. Hoogenboom, pp. 264–65.

CHAPTER THREE

1. Alexander Clarence Flick, *Samuel Jones Tilden* (Port Washington, N.Y.: Kennikat Press, 1963), p. 6.

2. Ibid., p. 5.

3. Donald B. Cole, *Martin Van Buren and the American Political System* (Princeton, N.J.: Princeton University Press, 1984), p. 369.

4. Biddle to Herman Cope, Biddle Correspondence, p. 256, quoted in Arthur M. Schlesinger, Jr., *The Age of Jackson* (Boston: Little, Brown & Co., 1946), p. 211.

5. Cole, p. 370.

6. Flick, p. 55.

7. Ibid., pp. 108–9.

8. Ibid., p. 130.

9. Ibid., p. 179.

CHAPTER FOUR

1. John Bigelow, ed., *Letters and Literary Memorials of Samuel J. Tilden,* vol. 2 (Port Washington, N.Y.: Kennikat Press, 1971), p. 439.

2. Quoted in Arthur M. Schlesinger, Jr., ed., *History of American Presidential Elections, 1789–1968,* vol. 4 (New York: Chelsea House Publishers, 1985), p. 1445.

CHAPTER FIVE

1. Quoted in Haworth, p. 45.

2. Ibid., p. 46.

3. Hoogenboom, p. 278.

4. Haworth, p. 318.

5. Ibid., p. 74.

6. Ibid., p. 76.

7. Ibid., pp. 85–86.

8. Quoted in James Ford Rhodes, *History of the United States,* vol. VII (Norwood, Mass.: Norwood Press, 1906), p. 231.

9. Ibid., pp. 241–43.

CHAPTER SIX

1. Quoted in Haworth, p. 200.

2. Milton Harlow Northrup, "The Inner History of the Origin and Formation of the Electoral Commission of 1877," *XL Century,* 1901, pp. 927, 928.

3. Quoted in Charles Warren, *The Supreme Court in U.S. History,* (Boston: Little, Brown & Co., 1923), vol. 3, p. 27.

4. Edward S. Corwin, "The Dred Scott Decision in the Light of Contemporary Legal Doctrine," *American Historical Review* XVII (1911), quoted in Warren, *The Supreme Court,* vol. 3, pp. 38–39.

5. *New York Times,* October 14, 1964, quoted in Warren, *The Supreme Court,* vol. 3, p. 114.

6. C. Peter Magrath, *Morrison R. Waite* (New York: Macmillan Publishing Co., 1963), p. 282.

7. 8 Wall. 603.

8. 12 Wall. 457.

9. Quoted in Magrath, p. 6.

10. Ibid., p. 12.

11. Ibid., p. 2.

12. Willard L. King, *Lincoln's Manager* (Cambridge, Mass.: Harvard University Press, 1960), p. 87.

13. Ibid., p. 141.

14. Quoted in King, p. 193.

15. Ibid., p. 201.

16. Ibid., p. 207.

17. Ibid., p. 258.

18. Ibid., p. 277.

CHAPTER SEVEN

1. Carl Brent Swisher, *Stephen J. Field* (Washington, D.C.: Brookings Institution, 1930), p. 2.

2. Ibid., pp. 116–17.

3. Ibid., p. 343.

4. Ibid., p. 348.

5. *In Re Nagle,* 135 U.S. 1, 75–76 (1890).

6. Swisher, pp. 125–26.

7. Quoted in Charles Fairman, *History of the Supreme Court,* vol. VII suppl. (New York: Macmillan Publishing Co., 1988), p. 252.

8. Ibid., p. 277.

9. Ibid., pp. 425–26.

10. *Strauder v. West Virginia,* 100 U.S. 303 (1879).

11. *New York Sun,* January 31, 1877, p. 1.

12. Quoted in Allison Dunham and Phillip B. Kurland, eds., *Mr. Justice* (Chicago: University of Chicago Press, 1956), p. 73.

13. *Murray v. Hoboken Land Co.,* 59 U.S. 272 (1856); 18 How. 272.

14. The Civil Rights Cases, 109 U.S. 3 (1883).

CHAPTER EIGHT

1. Fairman, *History of the Supreme Court,* pp. 56–57.

2. Quoted in Fairman, *History of the Supreme Court,* p. 65.

3. Ibid., p. 80.

4. *Proceedings of the Electoral Commission* (Washington, D.C.: Government Printing Office, 1877), p. 1001.

5. Ibid., p. 1007.

6. Ibid., p. 1014.

7. Quoted in Fairman, *History of the Supreme Court,* p. 95.

8. *Proceedings,* p. 1058.

9. Fairman, *History of the Supreme Court,* p. 112.

10. Quoted in Haworth, p. 258.

11. Ibid., p. 282.

CHAPTER NINE

1. James B. Bryce, *The American Commonwealth* (London: Macmillan & Co., 1889), p. 1.

2. King, p. 293, n. 23.

3. Fairman, *History of the Supreme Court,* p. 38.

4. Quoted in Fairman, *History of the Supreme Court,* p. 123.

5. *New York Sun,* July 6, 1977.

6. Ibid., August 4, 1877.

7. Fairman, *History of the Supreme Court,* p. 131.

8. Ibid., p. 132.

9. Ibid., pp. 132–33.

10. Ibid., pp. 135–36.

11. Allan Nevins, *Abram S. Hewitt* (New York: Harper & Brothers, 1935).

12. Ibid., p. 323.

13. Ibid., pp. 367–68.

14. Ibid., p. 372.

CHAPTER TEN

1. Flick, p. 403.

2. Quoted in Flick, p. 396.

3. Ibid., p. 396.

4. Ibid., p. 412.

5. *New York Herald,* February 10, 1879, quoted in Flick, p. 432.

6. *New York Times,* April 21, 1880, quoted in Flick, p. 450.

7. Quoted in Flick, p. 454.

8. Henry James Abraham, *Justices, Presidents, and Senators* (Lanham, Md.: Rowman & Littlefield Publishers, 1999), app. A.

EPILOGUE

1. Quoted in Magrath, p. 288.

2. Quoted in George Pellew, *John Jay* (New York: Chelsea House Publishers, 1980), p. 268.

3. Quoted in Willard L. King, *Melville Weston Fuller* (New York: Macmillan Publishing Co., 1950), p. 116.

4. Ibid., pp. 246–47.

5. Executive Order No. 8983, 6 Fed. Reg. 6569 (1941).

6. Quoted in Robert B. Stinnett, *Day of Deceit* (New York: Free Press, 2000), p. 235.

7. Quoted in Alpheus Thomas Mason, *Harlan Fiske Stone: Pillar of the Law* (New York: Viking Press, 1956), p. 581.

8. Telford Taylor, *The Anatomy of the Nuremberg Trials* (New York: Alfred A. Knopf, 1992), p. 634.

9. Quoted in Eugene C. Gerhart, *America's Advocate: Robert H. Jackson* (Indianapolis: Bobbs-Merrill Co., 1958), p. 440.

10. William O. Douglas, *The Court Years* (New York: Vintage Books, 1981), p. 28.

11. Quoted in Mason, p. 716.

12. Mason, p. 718.

13. Quoted in Gerhart, p. 441.

14. Earl Warren, *The Memoirs of Earl Warren* (Garden City, N.Y.: Doubleday & Co., 1977), p. 356.

15. Ibid., p. 358.

Bibliography

Abraham, Henry James. *Justices, Presidents, and Senators: A History of the U.S. Supreme Court Appointments from Washington to Clinton.* Lanham, Md.: Rowman & Littlefield Publishers, 1999.

Bain, David Haward. *Empire Express.* New York: Viking Penguin, 1999.

Bernstein, Richard B. "The Sleeper Wakes: The History and Legacy of the Twenty-seventh Amendment." *Fordham Law Review* 7 (December 1992): 497–557.

Bigelow, John. *Letters and Literary Memorials of Samuel J. Tilden.* Dallas, Tex.: Taylor Publishing Co., 1971.

Brown, Dee. *The Year of the Century: 1876.* New York: Charles Scribner's Sons, 1966.

Bryce, James B. *The American Commonwealth.* London: Macmillan & Co., 1888.

Cardozo, Benjamin N. *The Nature of the Judicial Process.* New Haven, Conn.: Yale University Press, 1921.

Cole, Donald B. *Martin Van Buren and the American Political System.* Princeton, N.J.: Princeton University Press, 1984.

Congressional Quarterly. *Presidential Elections: 1789–1996.* Washington, D.C.: Congressional Quarterly, 1997.

Dunham, Allison, and Philip B. Kurland, eds. *Mr. Justice.* Chicago: University of Chicago Press, 1956.

Everitt, Anthony. *Cicero.* New York: Random House, 2001.

Fairman, Charles. *History of the Supreme Court.* Vol. VII, suppl., *Five Jus-*

Bibliography

tices and the Electoral Commission of 1877. New York: Macmillan Publishing Co., 1988.

————. *Mr. Justice Miller and the Supreme Court 1862–1890*. Cambridge, Mass.: Harvard University Press, 1939.

Flick, Alexander C. *Samuel Jones Tilden: A Study in Political Sagacity*. Port Washington, N.Y.: Kennikat Press, 1963.

Friedman, Leon, and Fred L. Israel, eds. *The Justices of the United States Supreme Court, 1789–1978: Their Lives and Major Opinions*. Vol. II. New York: Chelsea House Publishing, 1980.

Hale, William Harlan. *Horace Greeley: Voice of the People*. New York: Harper & Brothers, 1950.

Hanna, Katheryn A. *Florida: Land of Change*. Chapel Hill, N.C.: University of North Carolina Press, 1948.

Haworth, Paul Leland. *The Hayes-Tilden Election*. Indianapolis: Bobbs-Merrill Co., 1906.

Hoogenboom, Ari. *Rutherford B. Hayes: Warrior and President*. Lawrence: University Press of Kansas, 1995.

King, Willard L. *Lincoln's Manager: David Davis*. Cambridge, Mass.: Harvard University Press, 1960.

Magrath, C. Peter. *Morrison R. Waite: The Triumph of Character*. New York: Macmillan Publishing Co., 1963.

Muzzey, David Saville. *James G. Blaine: A Political Idol of Other Days*. Port Washington, N.Y.: Kennikat Press, 1934.

Nevins, Allan. *Abram S. Hewitt: With Some Account for Peter Cooper*. New York: Harper & Brothers, 1935.

Niven, John. *Martin Van Buren: The Romantic Age of American Politics*. New York: Oxford University Press, 1983.

O'Malley, Michael. *Keeping Watch: A History of American Time*. New York: Penguin Books, 1990.

Perret, Geoffrey. *Ulysses S. Grant: Soldier and President*. New York: Random House, 1997.

Proceedings of the Electoral Commission and of the Two Houses of Congress in Joint Meeting Relative to the Count of Electoral Votes Cast December 6, 1876 for the Presidential Term Commencing March 4, 1877. Washington, D.C.: U.S. Government Printing Office, 1877.

Rhodes, James Ford. *History of the United States*. Vol. VII, *1850–1877*, Norwood, Mass.: Norwood Press, 1906.

Bibliography

Rinhart, Floyd, and Marion Rinhart. *America's Centennial Celebration: (Philadelphia, 1876)*. Winter Haven, Fla.: Manta Books, 1976.

Robinson, Lloyd. *Stolen Election: Hayes versus Tilden, 1876*. Garden City, N.Y.: Doubleday & Co. 1968.

Ross, Earle Dudley. *The Liberal Republican Movement*. New York: Henry Holt & Co., 1919.

Schlesinger, Jr., Arthur M. *The Age of Jackson*. Boston: Little, Brown & Co., 1946.

————, ed. *History of American Presidential Elections, 1789–1968*. Vol. IV. New York: Chelsea House Publishers, 1985.

Smith, Jean Edward. *Grant*. New York: Simon & Schuster, 2001.

Swanberg, W. A. *Sickles the Incredible*. New York: Charles Scribner's Sons, 1956.

Swisher, Charles B. *Stephen J. Field: Craftsman of the Law*. Washington, D.C.: Brookings Institution, 1930.

Taylor, Telford. *The Anatomy of the Nuremberg Trials*. New York: Alfred A. Knopf, 1992.

Tebeau, Charlton W. *A History of Florida*. Miami: University of Miami Press, 1971.

Trefousse, Hans Louis. *Carl Schurz: A Biography*. Knoxville: University of Tennessee Press, 1982.

Trimble, Bruce R. *Chief Justice Waite: Defender of the Public Interest*. Princeton, N.J.: Princeton University Press, 1938.

Weigley, Russell F. *Philadelphia: A 300-Year History*. New York: W. W. Norton & Co., 1982.

Woodward, C. Vann. *Reunion and Reaction: The Compromise of 1877 and the End of Reconstruction*. Boston: Little, Brown & Co., 1966.

Index

Note: Page numbers in italics refer to illustrations.

Index

Index

Frémont, John C., 10, 14, 72
Fuller, Melville W., 225–29, 246
Fulton, Robert, 8

Garfield, James A.:
  assassination of, 216
  and Electoral Commission, 163,
    164, 165, 168, 172, 175, 177,
    188, 195–96, 222, 248
  and Louisiana election results,
    102
  presidency of, 208, 213, 214–15
  and Supreme Court, 217
Garrett, John W., 205
Garrison, William Lloyd, 74
Godkin, Edwin L., 23
gold, price of, 18–20
gold standard, 206–7
Gordon, J. B., 178
Gore, Al, 3
Göring, Hermann, 238
Gould, Jay, 19, 20
Grant, Ulysses S., *153*
  Army career of, 11–14, 15, 116
  cabinet of, 15–16, 27, 29–31, 51,
    52, 97, 130
  at Centennial Exhibition, 8, 31
  and civil rights legislation, 18
  and civil service reform, 22
  death of, 216
  and 1868 election, 14–15, 24, 48,
    76, 80–81
  and 1872 election, 24, 95, 140–41
  and 1876 election, 4, 101, 102,
    108, 119, 189, 203
  and 1880 election, 213–14, 216
  and foreign affairs, 20–21, 49

as lame duck, 31, 141
and Panic of 1873, 24, 26, 79
political innocence of, 14, 15
presidency of, 9, 15–32, 114, 207
and public credit act, 18–20
ratings of, 31–32
scandals in tenure of, 18–20,
  24–25, 27, 28–31, 32, 49, 53, 78,
  84, 129
and soft money, 27, 79
and Supreme Court, 18, 28, 128,
  129–32, 155, 156, 160
and third term, 27, 50, 51
and Treaty of Washington,
  16–18
Great Britain:
  and Jay Treaty, 224, 225
  and Treaty of Washington,
    16–18
  and Venezuela boundary, 227,
    228–29, 246
Greeley, Horace, 23, 24, 118, 122,
  141
Green, Ashbel, 168
Greenback Legislation, 128, 156
Greenback Party, 26, 82–83
Greenleaf, Simon, 35, 37
Grier, Robert, 120, 122
Grover, L. F., 110, 111, 112
Guiteau, Charles, 216

Haiti, 20–21
Hale, Eugene, 102
Hall, Oakley, 77
Hamburg Massacre (1876), 108
Hamilton, Alexander, 222
Hampton, Wade, 108

Index

Index

Index

Stewart, Alexander, 16

Stokeley, William, 205

Stone, Harlan F., 234–36, 237,
240–41, 247

Story, Joseph, 35

Strauder v. West Virginia, 157

Strong, William:
  early years of, 156–57
  and Electoral Commission, 119,
    156, 158–59, 164, 170, 221, 222
  and Legal Tender Act, 128–29,
    156, 162
  newspaper articles against, 187
suffrage issues, 46, 48–49, 81, 105,
  106, 184

Summons, James, 38–39

Sumner, Charles, 16, 21, 45, 124

Supreme Court, U.S.:
  appellate jurisdiction of, 127–28,
    138, 217–18
  arguments before, 165
  Brown v. Board of Education,
    242
  Buchanan's appointments to, 123,
    145
  case load of, 138–39, 141, 217–18,
    225, 227
  Civil Rights Cases, 162, 217
  Cleveland's appointment to, 226
  conferences of, 197–98
  "diversity of citizenship" cases in,
    217–18
  Dred Scott case, 10, 74, 120–23,
    124, 132
  effect of member's absence in,
    240–41

and election of 1876, 114, 115,
  116–20, 132–33, 141
and election of 2000, 5–6
and Electoral Commission, 5,
  132–33, 143, 146, 153, 156,
  157–62, 220–22, 247–48
evaluation of, 218
Ex Parte Milligan, 126–27, 139–40
first century of, 119–20
first meeting of, 223
Garfield's appointment to, 217
Grant's appointments to, 18, 28,
  128, 129–32, 155, 156, 160
and habeas corpus, 152
Hayes' appointments to, 34,
  216–17
Hepburn v. Griswald, 128, 162
Hoover's appointment to, 231
Jackson's appointment to, 120
Knox v. Lee, 128–29, 156, 162
Lincoln's appointments to, 34,
  118, 123–25, 128, 135, 137–39,
  153, 154–55, 160
Madison's appointment to, 35
Murray v. Hoboken Land Co.,
  161
and other assignments, 40,
  125–26, 138, 140–41, 149,
  222–41, 242–47
secrecy in, 196
Slaughterhouse Cases, 149, 155,
  162
Strauder v. West Virginia, 157
supervision as role of, 123
tenth seat on, 148
trial judges from, 40

272

Index